"Art Up"
The Rebirth of a Dying Industry

By Donny "Goines" Scott

To everyone who thought I couldn't do it
And everyone who knew I could

The End of the Beginning

This story starts off where many end. As I sit in front of my computer, the thoughts of many things bounce around my skull like a silver metallic ball in an old pinball machine.

I need to pay my back rent.

I have to prepare for a defamation trial in small claims court.

I have no food in the fridge.

I'm over $20,000 dollars in the hole.

My company needs a new website.

I haven't released a new record in months.

I have one solitary quarter to my name. Literally.

I need my Clonazepam.

Obstacles such as these have broken many men, but I will not fall victim to the same fate. You can attribute this proclamation to my unwavering confidence, blind faith or the egotistical nature of a champion. Nevertheless, the future will be a testament to these words.

I will not fail.

Table of Contents

CHAPTER ONE: THE PHONE CALL
CHAPTER TWO: MOMENT OF CONCEPTION
CHAPTER THREE: THE MAKI FACTOR
CHAPTER FOUR: INTERVENTION
CHAPTER FIVE: BAND OF UNMERRY MEN
CHAPTER SIX: RELEASE
CHAPTER SEVEN: DONNY THE "C.E.O"
CHAPTER EIGHT: THE DECLAMA DRAMA

Chapter One: The Phone Call

Sometime late in July of 2011, I decided to visit my parents in Virginia. They had recently relocated there from New York and I always found the environment to be a relaxing contrast to the city that never sleeps. Neither did I. In fact, the only way I could sleep was by popping 30- to 40 milligrams of Ambien every night. I'm still afflicted by this issue, but eventually I will be able wing myself off of them. Hopefully. At least that's what Dr. Westmooreland (I'll give you one guess as to what her profession is...) tells me, but anyway I'm getting sidetracked.

My mother Donna Marie Lopez Adams and Pops (my Mothers husband) Clarence Adams are two of the nicest people you can ever meet. Sure, we've had our differences in the past. My years of alcoholism (maybe I'm being too harsh on myself but let's just say I drunk way too much) didn't help matters much either. I'm proud to say that I'm sober these days (minus the "legal" drugs) but I love being around them. They may not know it, but I've picked up many traits and characteristics from them. We've fought, cursed each out, cried together and everything else in between but as an adult I found them to be two of the truest friends I would ever find in this world. This story isn't about them though.

The phone call I would receive that fateful summer day from my now ex-manager Jonathan Master would change my perception of everything and everyone around me forever as an artist.

Jonathan is a very likeable guy. He Co-managed me with Jameel "Reality" Meeks, another great guy. Even though I eventually fired them, I still have love for them both to this day and we did some amazing things together. I can never take that away from them.

This particular phone call pertained to an album I was working on titled "Success Served Cold" which was an amazing project overall, but it could've been much better had we all worked as a team. I'll come back to that part much later though.

So as me and Jonathan would normally do during this time (planning promotional ideas months in advance) we began to talk about the album. It would feature legends such as Just Blaze, Bun B, Brother Ali and Killer Mike as well as newcomers like myself, Pill, XV, Laws, Jon Connor and many other artists that contributed that to that project. Although we all (Maki, Ariel, Juan, Juliet, Reality, Jonathan, Canei & Myself) had different ideas and opinions there was one collective thought no one could deny. It had major potential.

As we conversed, I expressed one major concern of mines. We needed to align with a very strong sponsor to make a huge impact. When I told Jonathan this, his reply to me was something to the effect of "Well, your brand isn't worth 10k..." in this calm but pompous tone he is well known for. I was stunned. I looked at my phone for a second and chose my next words (or word) very carefully. Why?

He gave me a list of all of these reasons that honestly made no sense to me. Sha Money XL didn't want to sign me, so and so didn't like my music (I tuned him out after the first part) and other things which I don't remember. We ended the call on a good note but I knew he would no longer be my manager anymore.

After that I spent a lot of time thinking about my next move. Honestly, it took a couple days to recover from that statement. We've had many heated arguments in the past but that one sentence hurt me the most. Even if his assumption was correct (which was proved wrong very shortly thereafter) as my manager and friend I felt let down. As far as I was concerned, he didn't believe in me anymore as an artist. I kept these thoughts to myself at the time and as always, kept on trucking as they say.

You see, the path I chose as an artist was a difficult one and I suffered many disappointments and losses along the way. A failed marriage to an amazing woman named Nathalie, my first born and only child Jesus Divine Rosario Scott's death, the suicide of my first mentor and a great friend Disco D…. My journey up to this point has been tortuous. It was grueling and full of stressors that would destroy the average human being. I almost lost my sanity truthfully (hence the Zoloft, Ambien, Clonazepam, Psychiatrist and extreme burst of emotions in either direction at times) but I suffered in silence and just continued on as I always do. Heartbroken, hurt, and exhausted in almost everyway imaginable but as far as the world was concerned I was "Donny Goines, the relentless go getter who always had a smile on his face…" The show must go on as they say right?

One thing that puzzled me about Jonathan's statement was that I had no ambition of signing a record deal. He knew that, I knew that and it made absolutely no sense to me whatsoever. It felt more like an excuse then a reason in my opinion but after I wrapped my mind around it a bit I decided to take matters into my own hands.

Chapter Two: Moment of Conception

From that experience an idea was born. It's hard to explain honestly, because it was more like a cultivation of many different factors that aligned simultaneously to forge what would later become Ink Different Inc.

I became possessed with this thought of "Ultimate Creative Freedom" as an artist. I started to do research. Maybe it's something innate within me, but I had already started the process of gathering intel month's prior. I had sit-downs with Murs and Just Blaze. Phone calls with everyone from Immortal Tech, Zach Katz, Chris from Koch, TJ Chapman and many more. Conversed via email with Brother Ali and Talib Kweli asking for advice. I didn't really want "anything" in particular expect knowledge and experience from those who I respect and have went through it.

The first thing I wanted to learn was how effective (or ineffective) certain online campaigns were. The first trial started with Adsense for Google and Facebook Ads. I used both for about a week to gauge the amount of exposure it would help me gain, to study the way people perceive things I said, how I was viewed publically and other data that would become very useful to me down the line.

The second test to see how "valuable" my talent was. So during this down time I did two different things to determine this. I launched a "verse" campaign for a bunch of various artists across the country. Surprisingly, that campaign was highly effective and I earned thousands of dollars. Even with the overhead (Studio time, traveling, etc.) it was a very successful experiment. The next one didn't do too well. In other words, it failed miserably.

I asked the fans to make donations if they supported my music. You see, I gave away so much music and tried to sell too little of it (Minute after Midnight album with Amalgam Digital and the Ich!ban single through Tunecore) I couldn't gauge if people would actually **PAY** for it. I got a few donations but they were modest in comparison.

I now knew I wanted to start my own company so I wrote a private email to a few of my colleagues asking for their help. A few did, but mainly didn't which lead me to my next thought. Writing formal proposals to major companies for support.

At the time, I wasn't too sharp with these and usually would rely on Jonathan to put them together but since I no longer wanted to hear his opinion I learned how to do them on my own. It wasn't that hard once I got the hang of it. These days I can write 10 different proposals in one day if need be, but back then my pace was much slower.

I was always good with verbal communication, which is how I broke through many barriers early on in my career but this method would take a little verbal finesse. I always prided myself in being a lyricist, and as you can tell from my stage name am an avid reader so I knew it wouldn't pose much of a problem.

The first people I targeted were major clothing and footwear companies. In fact, I only went after two. Artful Dodger (which was owned by Iconix and Jay Z) and Adidas. I chose the first one based on an impromptu visit to the office with my homegirl DSY.

I met Just C and Sain, who were both in charge of the brand's development and instantly knew they, would be great people to work with.

I liked their style, attitude and vibe so I expressed interest and they jumped on board. This boosted my confidence tremendously because according to my manager my brand wasn't worth 10k but now I had the support of a million dollar company. In fact, the album would end up being sponsored by Rocawear **AND** Artful Dodger. That knocked Jonathan's theory out the box.

Adidas was (and still is in my opinion) a company that always manages to stay ahead of the curve. I studied their movements for years and I really liked the campaigns they worked with artists such as B.O.B for example, so I decided to reach out to them as well.

I hate Twitter. If you follow me you would probably think otherwise, but these days it's a necessary evil so I utilize it. Little known fact, I was going to do a social media "black out" (erasing my Twitter, Facebook, etc.) but at the very last minute decided against it due to one factor. My supporters. Someone pointed out something to me that I didn't really think about during the time. Someone said they thought it would be a selfish act because people want to know what's going on with me. I agreed. The people have, and always will come first to me.

One thing Twitter is good for (besides finding out who Kim Kardashian is dating and what Justin Bieber ate for lunch. Don't you just love obvious sarcasm? Anyway...) though is research. So with a litter recon work I found the person I should be speaking to. Jon Wexler.

I liked Jon right from the start and we still converse regularly to this date. I pitched him a clever idea for a campaign he loved and it was actually green lit but somehow fell through. It happens, but the lesson learned from that experience was that executives took me seriously.

This played an important factor in the next proposal, which was the "The Big Lebowski" (Shut the f#ck up Donny! was a common joke during the recording process and we even thought about using it for a song on the album), as I would say. iTunes.

That situation is confidential so I legally can't discuss it but now I knew how to break free and saw the light at the end of the tunnel. Now I begun to take measures to ensure I would be in a good space upon my exit.

Many people asked me, "What does the title of your album mean?" and I always had to break it down. It's almost prophetic in a sense. It's basically two different sayings combined. The first, Revenge is a dish best served cold. The Second, Success is the best revenge.

I never wanted to be an "overnight" celebrity. That's why I make the kind of moves I do. It's all about building a solid foundation and becoming the man I need to be in order to be able and handle that moment when it does arrive. It's not a matter of "if" at this point, it's more like when.

As I created this album, I wanted to show the world a glimpse of what to expect and that's exactly what I did. I have about 10 more of those in me. All I can say, be prepared to eat well in the very near future

Chapter Three: The Maki Factor

Maki was a producer who I met through Ariel when Just Blaze merged forces with Stadium Red. He brought with him Juan, Andy and the Greek Mystique himself. From day one Maki and me clicked. I've always liked him and he would eventually become the Executive Producer alongside Ariel.

I enjoyed talking to him about music, life and many other things in general and we hung out a lot. We shared many of the same traits personality wise and instantly became friends. Even though we would eventually have a falling out due to this album I still consider him a great man, immense talent and true friend.

During this time period I had also made a major decision that would change the course of my career and life dramatically. Earlier that year I was invited to down to Atlanta by my homie Mike from SMKA Productions (real good people) to perform for their upcoming release which I was featured on. As part of the promotion, we went to a studio called Treesound. I walked inside with the homie Laws and he introduced me to The Justice League (great producers and really humble dudes) and Roxy Reynolds (she looks AMAZING in person fellas) but the person who change my perspective on things that night was Groove Chambers. By far, one of the coolest dudes in the game I've ever met. After a cypher with Young Scolla, Rittz and more we started to build and he invited me down to record and work in the studio.

Two weeks later I was back down there and didn't bother using my return flight. I lived in the studio for a few months and occasionally stayed with my homegirl Shika from Harlem, who had relocated here for school a year prior.

Funny enough, I applied for an apartment in the building where she lived, not expecting to get approved but am now writing this book on the 32nd floor of a penthouse (more about her, this building and others later). It's funny how life plays out sometimes. I truly believe everything happens for a reason. Negative and Positive. Anyway, the people I met at Treesound will forever hold a place in my heart. Mali, 3 Little Digs, the entire staff are all great people and I can't thank them enough for the opportunity they gave me.

During the first week there I found out terrible news, of all places on Worldstar (I stopped visiting the site from that day on because I was just so appalled by what I had seen). There was a video posted on there regarding a shooting a Brighton Beach back in New York. Five people were shot and one person died. Her name was Tysha Jones.

I'm numb to death. Almost fully desensitized due my upbringing and environment. Someone getting murdered happens to be a normal occurrence in any ghetto of the world and it's just a way of life. This particular situation hit too close to home though. Tysha was the daughter of one of my very good friends Kevin and I literally watched that girl grow up in front of my eyes. I remember walking out of the studio, wandering for a few miles as tears slowly dripped down my face. I just felt so helpless, weak, hurt and disgusted by this act of senseless violence and had no desire to return back to my home unless I could help to change it. I went back to the studio and just kept a smile on my face. I was crying inside though. One thing I've learned to do throughout the years is hide my true emotions if needed.

I vowed to myself from that day forward I would be apart of the solution, and not a contributor to the issues the affect my community.

Coincidently, I had a session scheduled the next day with another good friend of mines named Simon Illa of Zac's recordings. He had sent me a beat prior but I wrote nothing to it. I woke up the next morning and words just started to emerge from the darkness within, and I wrote a song dedicated to her within a very short amount of time. We recorded the song and I put it right out. Not for publicity, not for money but for my people. For Kevin, for his family, for the countless lives lost which will never be found again. Most of all, I did it for myself. Music has always been a cathartic process for me and without it, I would've been dead or in jail at this point. I'm sure of it. Came close a few times actually, but I suppose my purpose hasn't been served yet.

I remember trying to reach out to Russell Simmons, Al Sharpton, the music community and everyone I could possibly think of to help me spread this message but to no true avail. I want to personally thank Peter Rosenberg for playing the record on the Hot 97 morning show because that truly meant a lot to his family and myself. I learned one thing from that situation. Nobody truly cares. It only matters when it matters to them. I personally will not sit by idle as chaos such as this ravishes my community. My world.

I often tell people, "I'm a man first, an artist second." It's deeper then that though. I'm a human being. Black or White. Young or Old. Woman or Man. Gay or Straight. No matter what you are or how anyone else may classify you as, you are a human. You are my brothers, my mothers, my cousins, my family and I love you.

That's why I fight so hard; it's the duality within in me. I'm a kind man of Mankind.

These factors equated to a problem I wasn't sure I could solve. I came down to work on music but my heart sank deep into an ocean of thoughts never emerging. I couldn't truly concentrate on the matters at hand, which brings me back to Maki.

Now, before I left New York, I was under the impression that the majority of my parts (vocals, concepts, etc.) were done but apparently I was wrong. You see Maki is a perfectionist with his music. Almost to the point of insanity and his constant requests to change lyrics, rerecord entire songs or verses and many other things really began to wear on me mentally. On top of this, he was worried about too many things pertaining to the project. He was concerned about everything from my management's involvement to the promotion, the usage of studio, the features and my presence missing in New York during the mixing process. Before I jump into this part though, let me backtrack a bit so you can get a better understanding of the entire situation.

I've worked with Ariel Borujow of Westward Music Group for years at this point. I first came to him a client when he had a modest studio under a bakery in Queens, and followed him to a then much smaller, Just Blaze-less environment called Stadium Red in Harlem. I had %110 faith in him and viewed him as a great friend, mentor and brother. I love Ariel still to this day, even after we fell out. I championed him and sang his praises to whoever would listen to my horrible singing voice (humor heals) but I never thought in a million years that he would eventually turn against me.

Chapter Four: Intervention

So apparently, back in the city of insomnia there were secret "meetings" going on. Topic of discussion? The lack of my sanity. Now I'll be the first one to tell you, I am **BEYOND** crazy but I'm far from insane. There is a difference.

Now that the project was nearing it's completion, and growing concerns of a few rusty screws apparently loosened I decided to go duck hunting (kill a few birds... I'm a rapper remember?) and hop on a flight back to New York. The plan was to have a collective "meeting of the mines", basically what I thought would be a short discussion about the responsibilities of each individual and address some concerns while I did a short promo run to promote the album. This was not that.

The meeting took place sometime during early September and my schedule was jammed packed. I hit the ground running and performed the night I landed. The meeting was scheduled for 8pm the next evening. Mind you, I (Donny Goines, not anyone else) had planned and secured many prominent media appearances and events. MTV, Karamloop, Rocawear Office Performance, Sirius radio interviews, the works. In fact, the night of the meeting that took place on a Monday I had two Sirius radio appearances (I sincerely apologize to Ron Mills, Ms. Mimi and Q for missing those interviews) scheduled at 9pm so my time was limited. I made sure to explain that to everyone and assumed this would be a very quick discussion. I wasn't prepared for what happened next.

I walked into an ambush. Juliet, Ariel, Maki, Jonathan, Reality, Juan and myself the *"Looney"*. I decided before I went in there to leave whatever preconceived ideas I had conjured up at the door. I sat down and it had begun. Compliant, after complaint, after complaint about something or the other. Everyone said I made them look bad based on my Paypal idea, Jonathan and Reality felt left out because they didn't hear the final version of a thank you record (which actually included them, but the version they heard omitted their names momentarily due to Maki arranging the record), Maki complaining about whatever, so on and so forth. Truthfully I don't remember everything that was said, but I do remember the feeling of being "set up" for a lack of better words. It felt more like an intervention then a meeting.

I didn't say a word at first. I let everyone speak and then started to address each issue individually (remember I was under time constraints?) as calm and as rational I could but eventually I just lost it. Somewhere down the line of speaking I lashed back out at all of them. I had complaints as well. Jonathan and Reality had secured NO beats, features, promotion, nothing!!! They got the worst of it. Ariel, who in my opinion was star struck at the time because of Just Blaze and all the extra awareness around the studio was slacking and not mixing any records. Nor did he get the Saigon feature he swore up and down he would. Maki was just getting on my nerves tremendously at this point due to his worrisome nature. For some reason he was always paranoid about something, his relationship with Just Blaze, how he was perceived in the public eye, his music and such. To both their credit, Juliet and Juan were the most levelheaded people in the room that night but it turned into an all out war in Studio A.

The only two things I remember after that? Firing my management the next day or so and missing both my Sirus radio show interviews. Livid is not a strong enough word to define how I felt that evening. The morale of the project was now gone as well.

Even though I didn't know how everything would play out in the end, I had a good idea but like always I just kept working.

You see, the work has always been the base of my sanity. It has kept me going during some of the worst moments of my life and honestly that's where my true power lies. I can endure. The Military trained me, the streets groomed me and life had created the man you see today. Many of you will never see me complain or cry but I do both. Quite often in fact. My soul has been stomped and stampeded upon many times, my heart's been broken and shattered repeatedly and my mind is in constant conflict with it.

Work, by sheer definition states; exertion or effort directed to produce or accomplish something; and in essence just means labor. That word describes the meaning quite accurately. Think about it. When a woman is going into "labor" she is giving birth to a seed planted months ago. She has to push and push to produce something she has been cultivating for nine months. The end result is a beautiful life brought to existence and that's kind of how I view my work. My hunger is insatiable and I will continue to strive for greater heights as I climb insurmountable obstacles in the eyes of others. To me though, they are just mere stepping-stones.

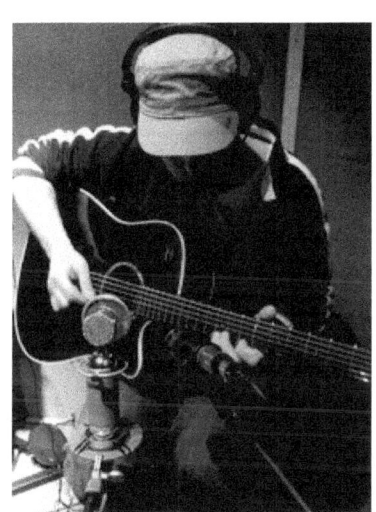

Maki creating...

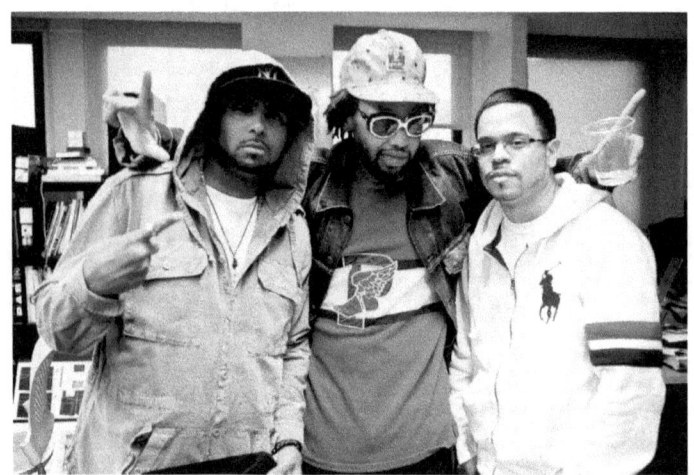

Myself, Polo and Juan at Rocawear offices

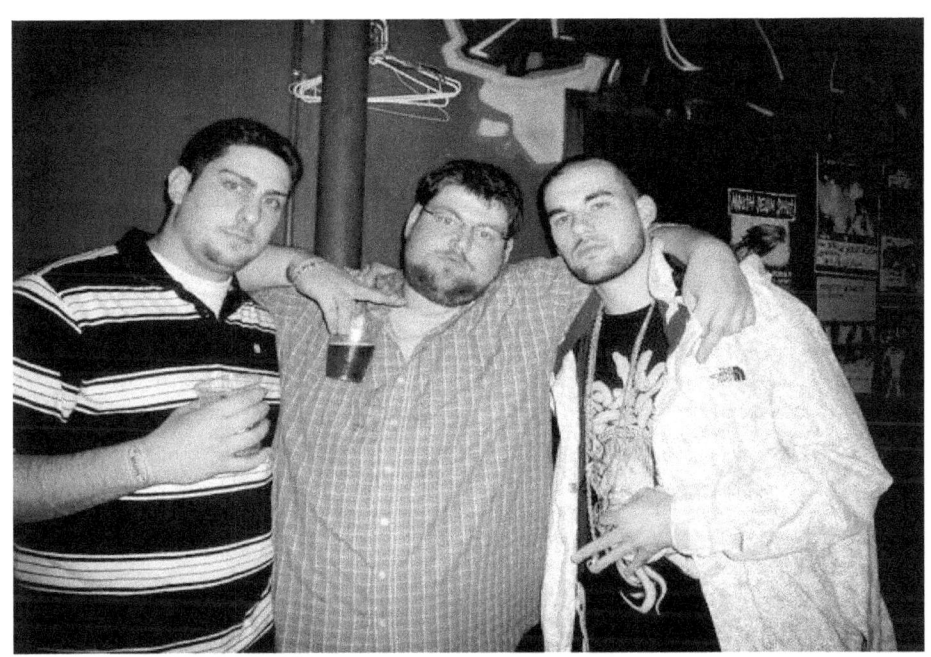

Adam, Jonathan and J the S

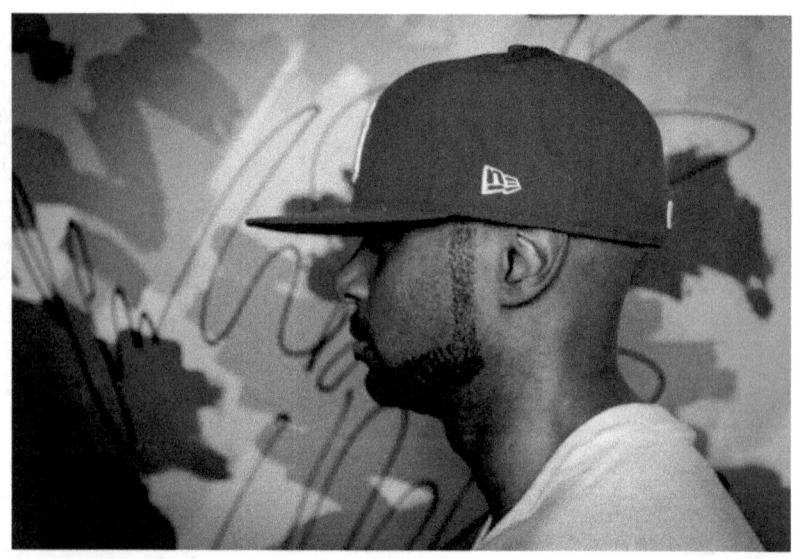
Art

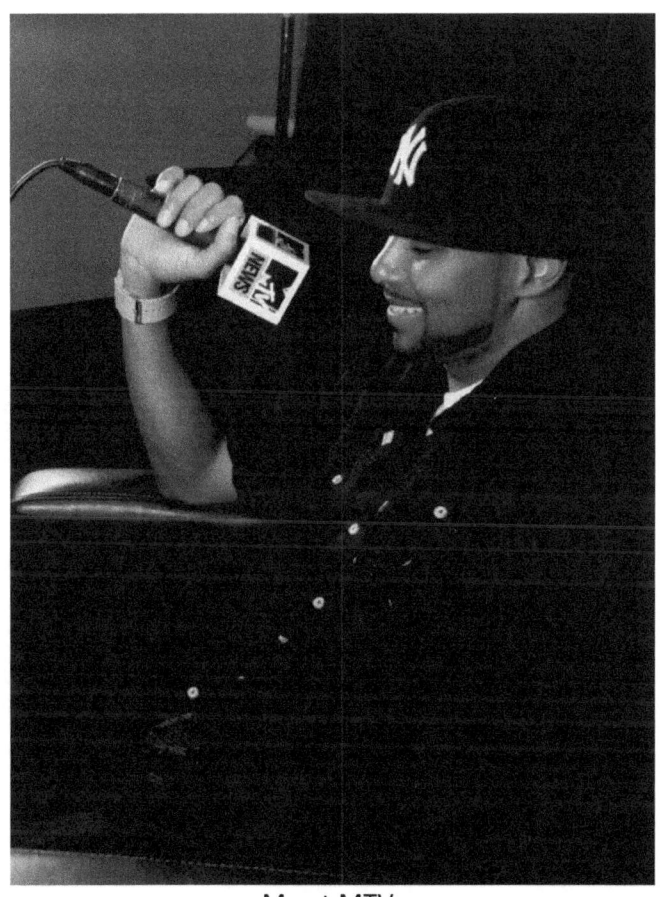
Me at MTV

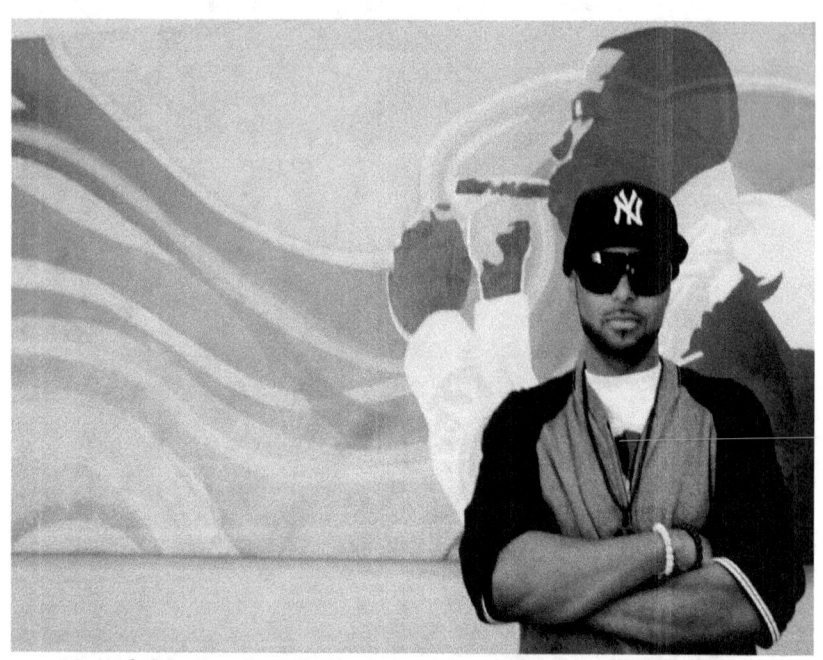

One of the very last times I would step foot in Stadium Red

#DONNYGOINES
#SSC
#ROCAWEAR
#ARTFUL DOGER
#DIGIWAXX

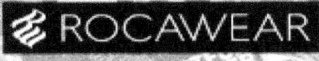 ROCAWEAR

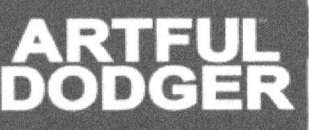 **ARTFUL DODGER**

CLUSTERFUCK
FRIDAYS

LIVE PERFORMANCE BY

DONNY
GOINES
#SUCCESS SERVED COLD

SPECIAL GUEST:
SKINNI SONNI

DATE 9/16/11
TIME 6PM TO 8PM
RSVP SAINWORLDENT@GMAIL.COM

B.Y.O.B 21 & OVER

DIGIWAXX

Clusterf#ck

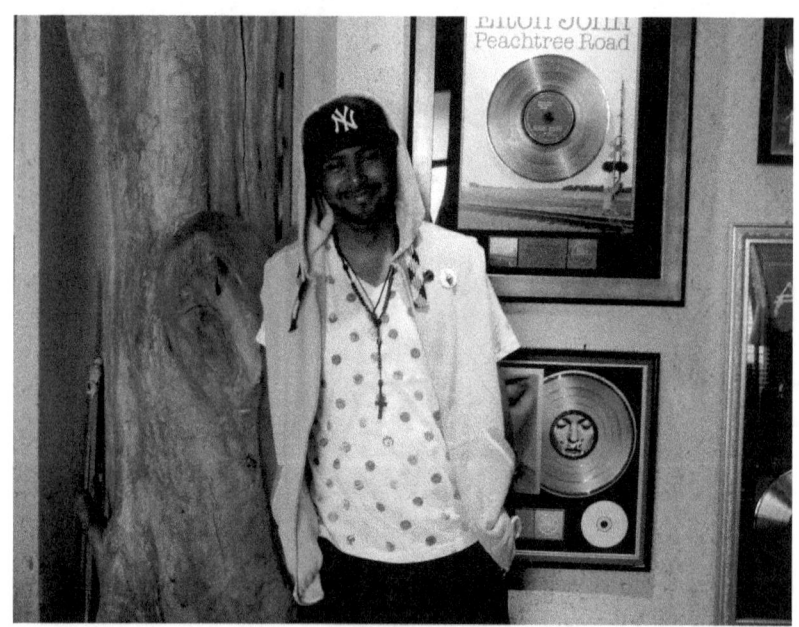

Me at the Tree

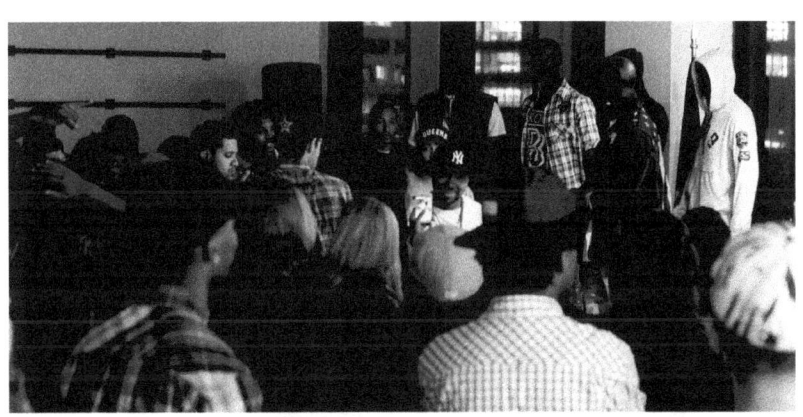

Another great performance

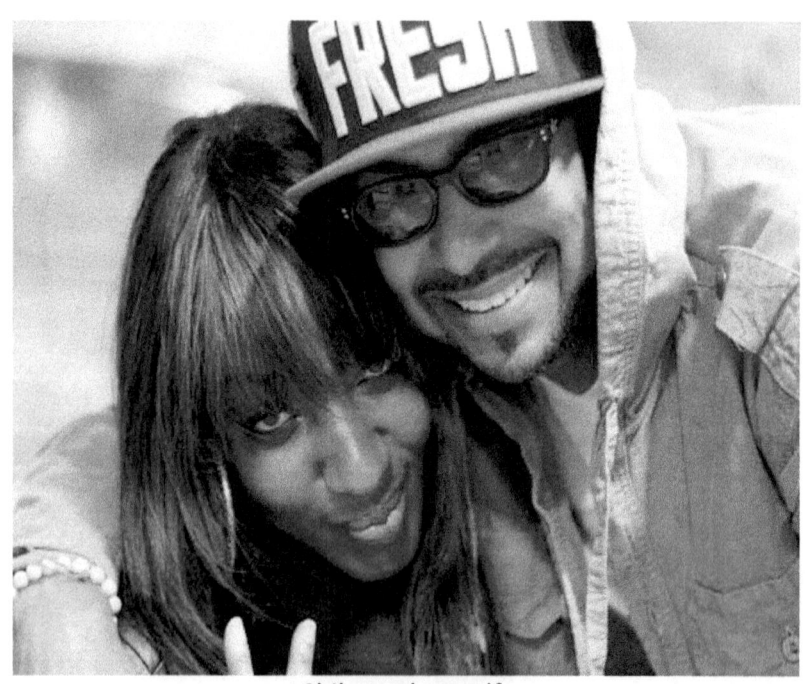

Shika and myself.
She doesn't know it but
I've always found her to be a
inspiring woman and
always liked her

1) End of the Prologue
   [Prod. by Maki]
2) Thought You Should Know feat. Mike Milan
   [Prod. by Canei Finch]
3) Barbarians feat. Just Blaze, Jon Connor, & Laws
   [Prod. by Frequency]
4) Ichiban Rmx feat Fred the Godson & Statik Selektah
   [Prod. by F.R.E.A.K.]
5) The Loudest Silence feat. Tess and Aja Monet
   [Prod. by Disco D]
6) Mountain of Memories feat. Brother Ali
   [Prod. by Canei Finch]
7) Liar feat. Lenny Harold
   [Prod. by Maki]
8) Black Noise
   [Prod. by Maki]
9) Champion's Anthem feat. Bun B, XV, Pill & Killer Mike
   [Prod. by Maki]
10) Prologue of the End
   [Prod. by Grand Staff]
11) Thank You feat. Emma Walker
   [Prod. by Maki]

Additional production:
Canei, additional arranging on "The Loudest Silence"
Beewirks, additional strings & horns on "The Loudest Silence"
Emma Walker, additional vocals on The Loudest Silence"

Musicians on "Thank You", Pete Arethene Jr. (drums), Jimmy Valentin (piano), David Shakespeare Vladimir Lindor (bass)
album artwork by Francis Vallejo

www.successservedcold.com

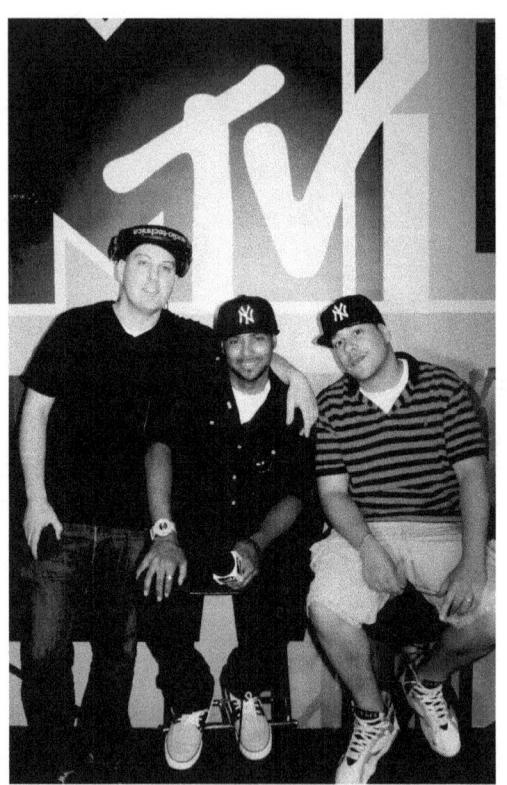

Maki, Myself and my bro Rob

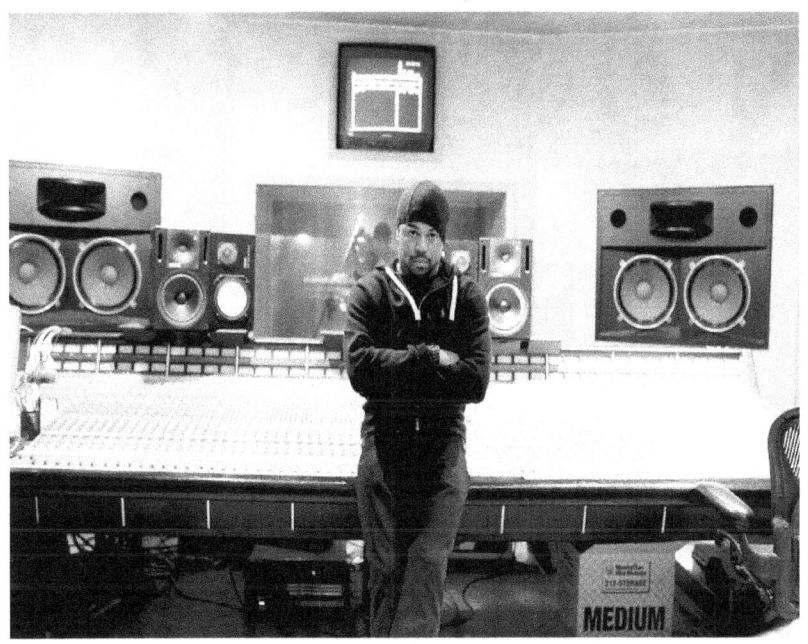

Legendary

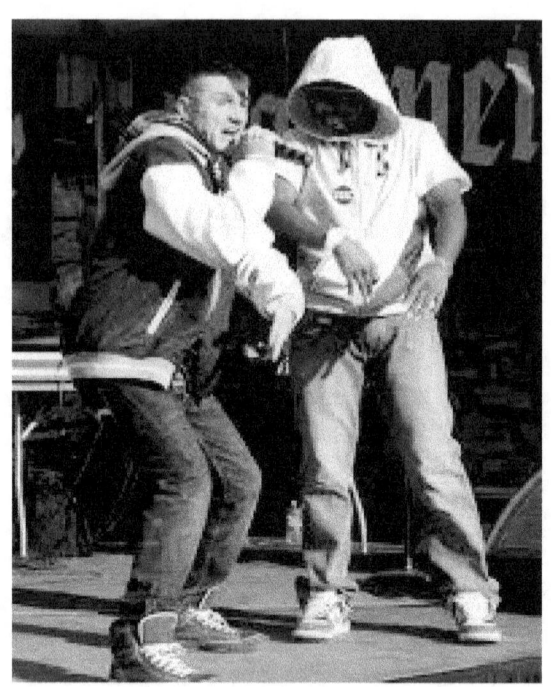
Me & Catch at A3C (Read on...)

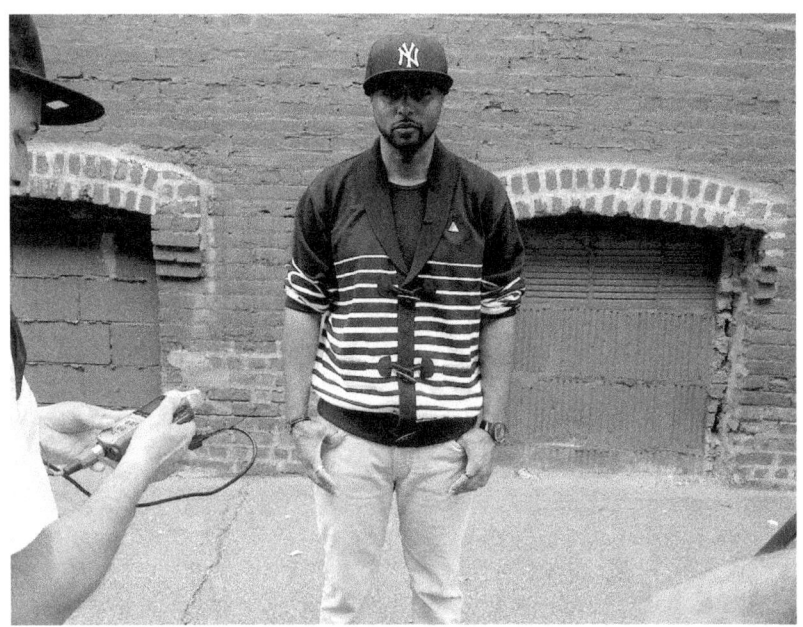

BET Shoot. Jose and all my BET fam. What up!!!!

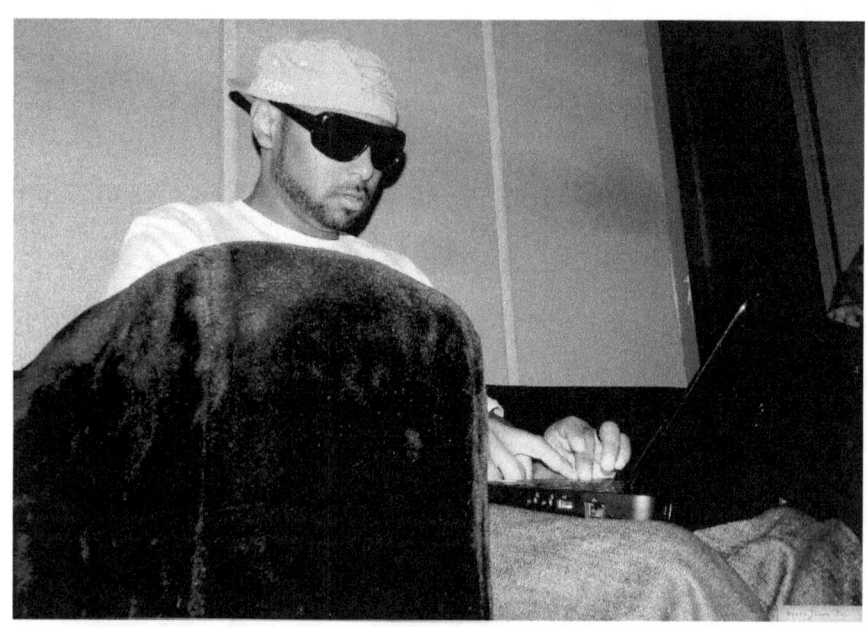

Me writing the song for Tysha Jones at Zac's Recording

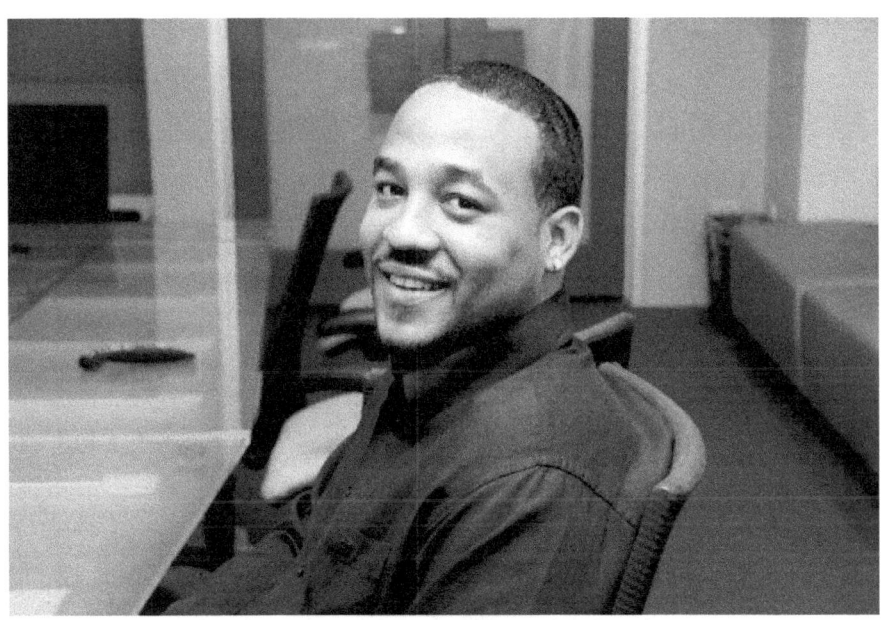

Reality (He always has a smile on his face)

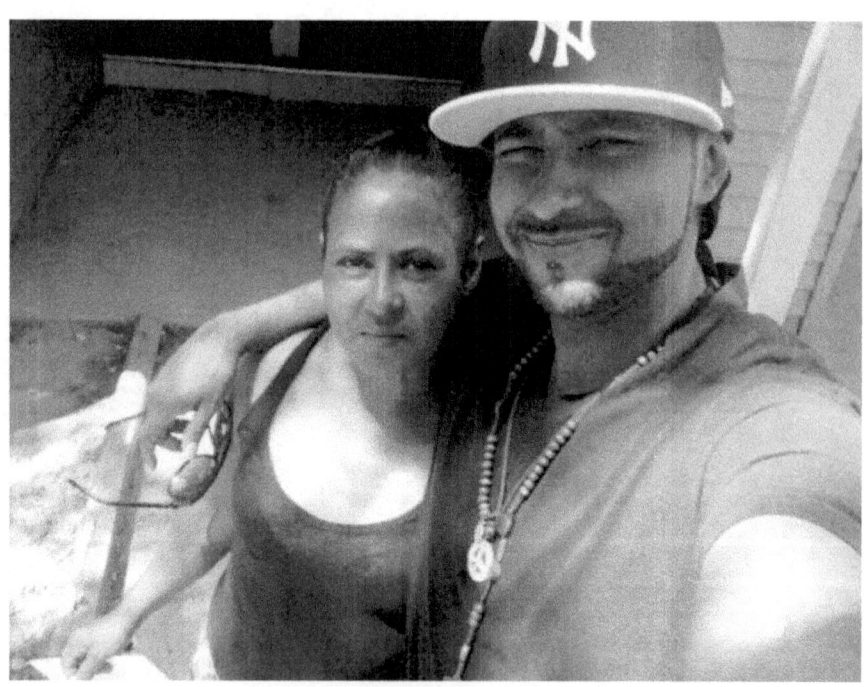

Me and my Mother (I do it for her)

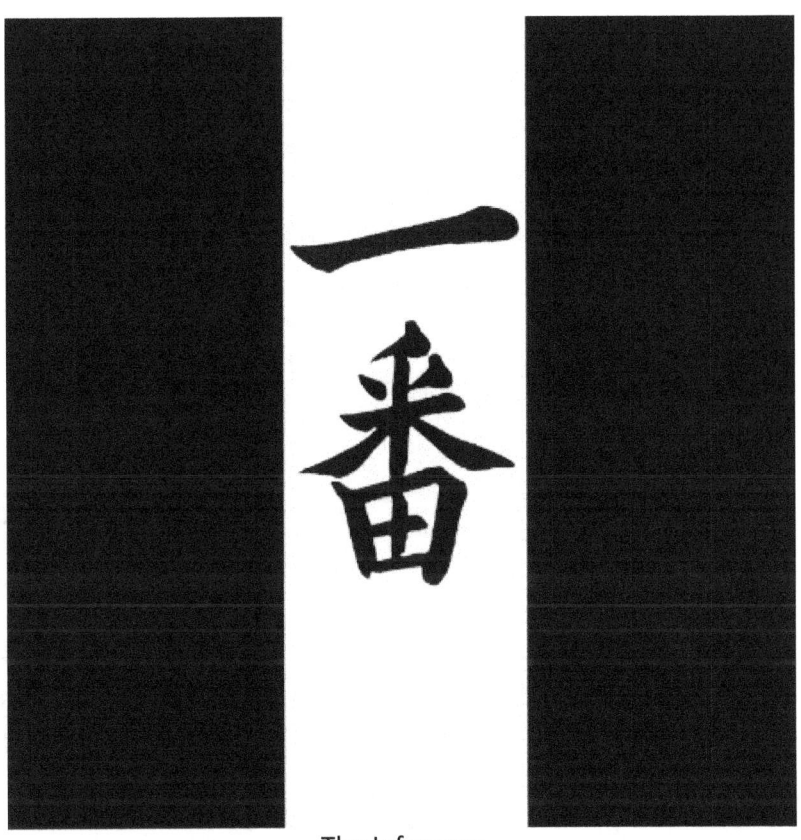

The Infamous

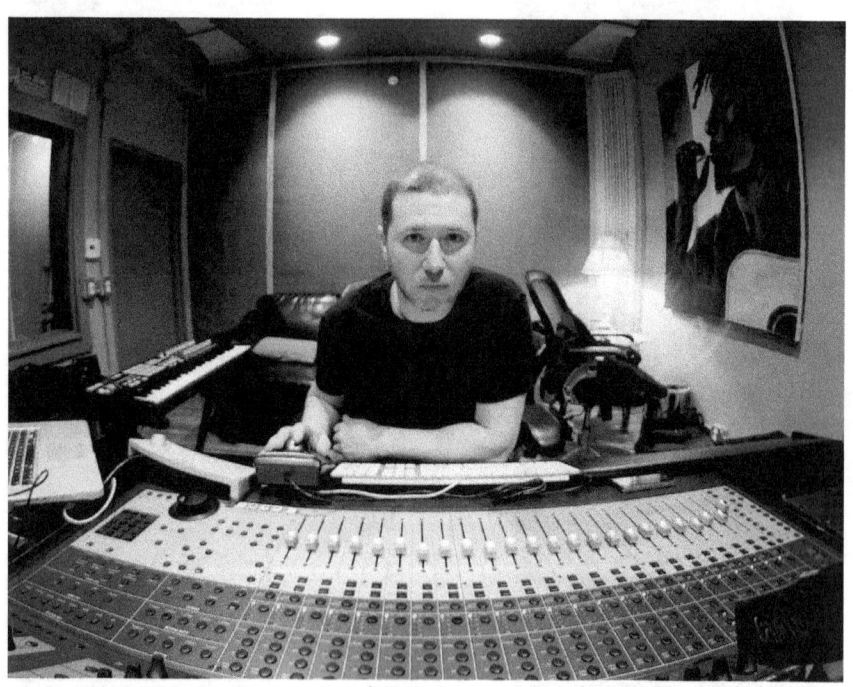

Ariel Borujow

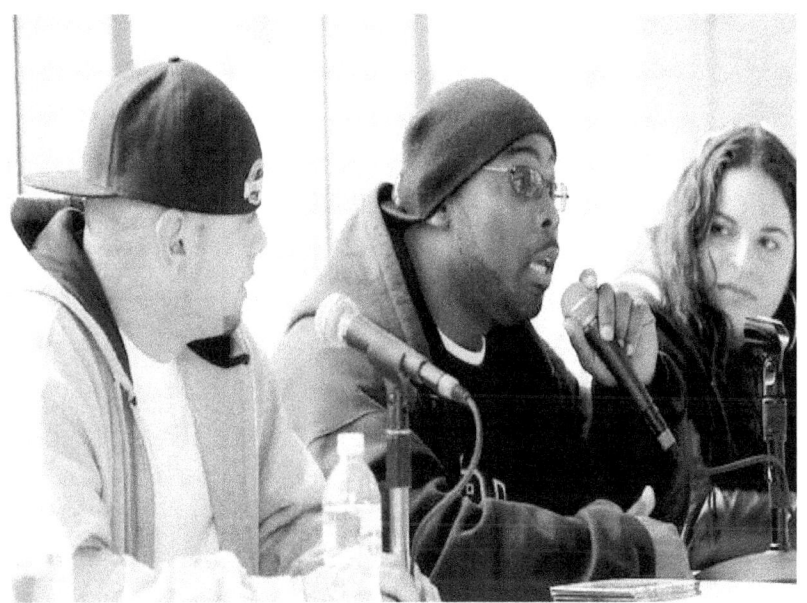
Juliet (to the far left) speaking on a panel

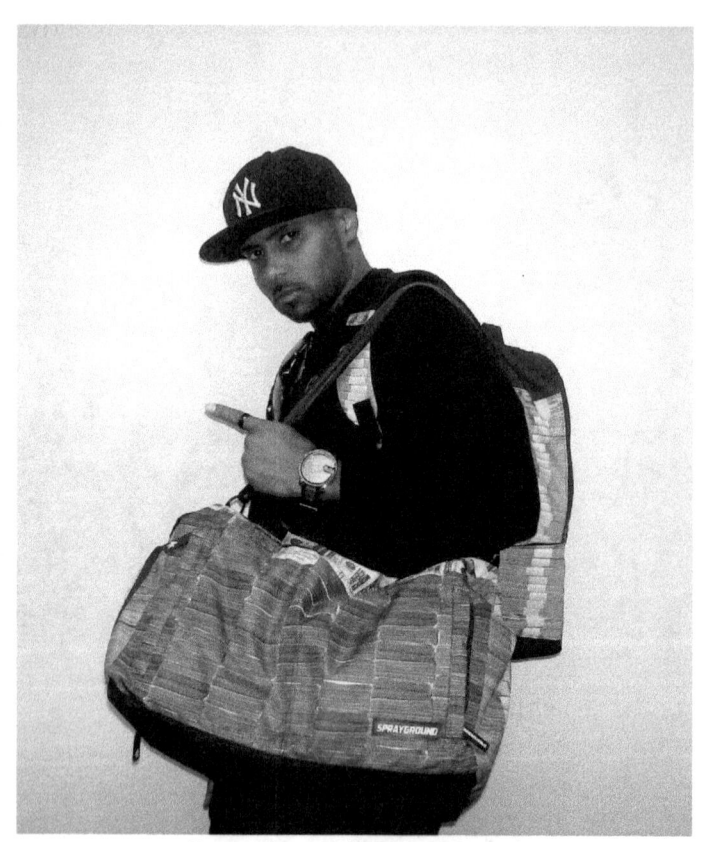

Campaign with Sprayground

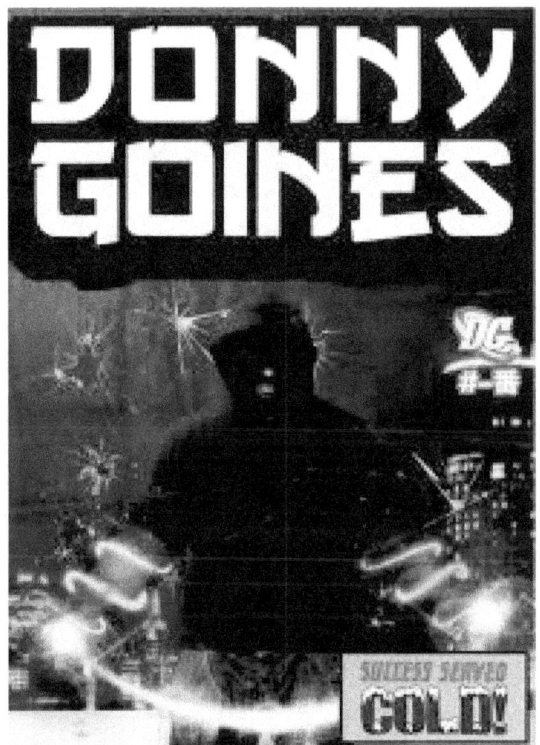

First version of album cover

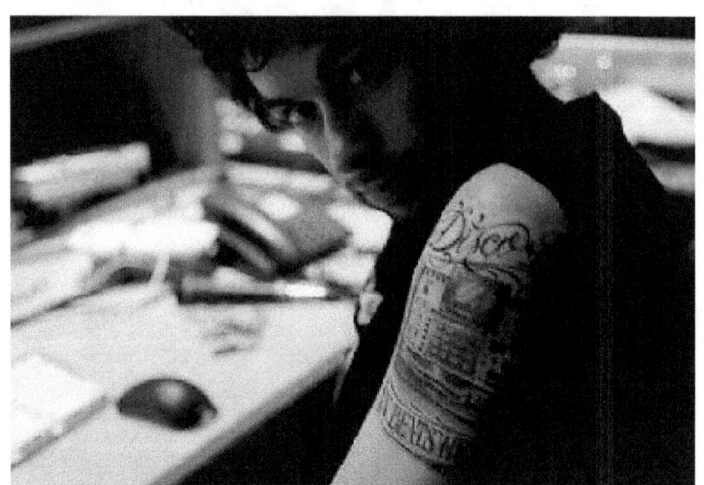

David "Disco D" Shayman

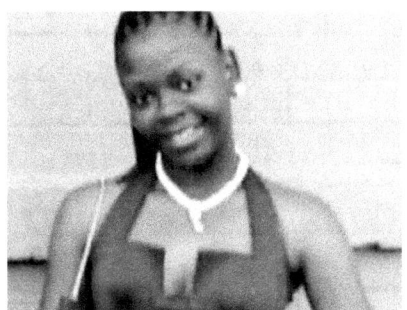

Tysha Jones

Chapter 5: Band of UNmerry Men

As far as the public was concerned, everything was coming along great and they were very excited to see the outcome of it all. Behind the scenes though there was a lot of tension and turmoil in the air. Regardless, the audience could never know. One thing I've learned throughout the years is the "P.T Barnum approach" as I like to call it. I study men like him, Harry Houdini and other legendary showman of all eras meticulously. They are great examples of what true showmanship entails. I don't study the Drakes of the world for example, because in my opinion they may get a page or two when it's all said and done but I need at least a chapter. Now back to the story at hand.

I continued on with my first promo run, now without my management. No offense to them, but I've always been capable of doing things on my own so it was no problem for me to move accordingly. I took helm of this ship with a Christopher Columbus type of naiveté. I didn't know where I was going exactly, but I knew there was much more land to find. I accomplished everything I needed to get done on that trip. Even picked up ANOTHER sponsor by the name of Sprayground. I hit up every magazine I could (invited or not) to make them aware of the upcoming project. Recorded all unfinished vocals for the album, conducted features with MTV, BET, Kamaloop TV and other major outlets. Lined up for more interviews and shows (including in office performances at Fader and Vibe which never panned out though), performed in the Rocawear building to give a sneak peek of the album and mini performance. Funny story about that one though...

I remember being in one of the offices rehearsing a song (I'm notorious for forgetting lyrics) and Maki came in and told me that Jay Z was here. My exact words to him were "I don't give a f#ck, I'm rehearsing". I know what you're thinking. Is this guy out of his mind? Not at all, in fact I am completely logical. Don't get me wrong, Jay Z was the catalyst to my career (Fade to Black sparked the flamed) and I have the utmost respect and admiration for him. My supporters come first though. Always. I wasn't there to rub shoulders with him; I was there to give an amazing performance for my upcoming album. I'm sure a man of his stature and accomplishment would understand my thought process without any further explanation, and if you are a person who is dedicated to his or her craft so will you.

Now that things were slightly calm I headed back to Atlanta to get settled in my new apartment. I moved into a one-bedroom apartment of a luxury building in Sandy Springs. Nice, modest, I liked it. I didn't have much when I got there except for artwork. I was content though. I slept on the floor for a few months deciding my next moves. The peacefulness engulfed me with the sort of comfort you would find under a blanket. Tranquil, peaceful and **SILENT!!!** I realized something critical in that apartment. I need silence in order to have piece of mind. I think it was a combination of many different factors. Living in New York City almost my entire life, running around the decaying apple countless nights, finding myself any and everywhere doing everything, the annoyances of living with my family. It all came to a boiling point but now started to simmer down. I felt great.

As for everyone else, it seemed like total anarchy. Ariel had no time to mix the project really. Juliet explained that business came first and I understood that.

I asked them for a release date (mind I had put out the first single for this album in January of that year) and they finally agreed by date of Nov 15th it would be mixed and mastered. So now I went even HARDER for promotion. We released the first single called "Champion's Anthem" that featured Bun B, Killer Mike, Pill, XV and DJ Corbett. Maki produced an amazing backdrop to a ridiculous record that should've put the wheels in motion. Zero to Sixty status (and it got up to about thirty I'd say) but without financial resources to shoot a video or push the record on a higher plateau we could only do but so much with it. Maki was nervous, I tried to calm him down but to no avail. I spoke to Juan to see if he could help him relax a bit and that did little to help so I decided to make one final trip to NY to put the nail in the coffin. Here's where everything became confusing.

Put yourself in my position. You have an amazing album ready to drop. Me, Maki, Perry, Phil, Ariel, Ricardo, Juliet and (all the artists who contributed) worked very hard on this project and wanted to see results. We are getting closer to the deadline and I am in charge of **EVERYTHING** promotional wise. Ariel never got Saigon and the last feature (who to be honest, was not even my idea) was the Just blaze intro to a record called "Barbarians" featuring Jon Connor and Laws. Maki proposed the idea but seemed afraid to ask him, so I took it upon myself to handle it. Like I always do. Maki went ballistic. To his defense I can understand why to some degree, but where I'm from scared money don't make money. I had never intended on asking Just Blaze for a beat or feature, and I am a **HUGE** fan of his. I think he is one of the greatest producers of all time, but I didn't want to impose upon him in that manner. I liked him as a person, and didn't care for all the hoopla and such. I was just listening to my Executive Producer.

Now this is the part none of you saw. I considered all of these people family, especially Ariel, Juliet & Claude. They had supported me for years in my endeavors and I can never thank them enough for that, no matter what happened after the facts. I've been working with these people for years and Ariel, most of all I considered a brother. So the events that transpired next really hurt me.

I had sponsors, and yes they were spending money to help push the product but none of it touched my hands. I had proposals in the air trying to get capital for this album to help make it successful but nothing was coming through at the time. I was under immense pressure from Maki, who had just has much incentive in this album as I did. I was told that after this project, Ariel would have to focus on other projects and such so he wouldn't be able to work with me as much in the near future. Which is totally understandable. They have overhead and things they want to do for their careers and I had no objections to anything whatsoever. However, this didn't solve the problem of finances. So I decided to ask Claude for a formal meeting to propose an idea to him. He agreed.

Claude is the owner of Stadium Red Studios. He is by far, one of the smartest and coolest men I've ever come across thus far and I respect him for his business savvy, tenacious work ethic and incredible foresight. I watched him build Stadium Red to what it is today and applaud him for that. Honestly, Claude is one impressive guy.

We sat down and I explained everything, which he understood. All he asked for was a formal business plan from me, which I delivered to him the next morning.

After a few weeks he turned me down, stating that he saw no real profit in the idea I proposed. That was cool. I'm use to hearing people telling me no but what happened next just seemed very strange. As a friend, I asked him for a loan of $1000 or something to that effect and his response was "You know I have to tell Julie about this right?" I was literally perplexed by that statement and didn't understand what he meant by it. I got the message the next day though, loud and clear.

Juliet sent me this formal email stating that after this project was mixed we could no longer work together. She explained how "appalled" she was that I circumvented them and went directly to Claude, and also how I was totally in the wrong in the matter. Honestly, I didn't even bother to fight back. I just texted her and said fine, whatever debt I owe you send it to me and I will pay in due time. She refused and absolved my debt then and there. I felt like someone had just plunged a machete right between my shoulder blades. This moment was by far the most one of the most disappointing in my life. Music aside.

First off, I consider Claude a friend so I never thought there was anything wrong with this situation. Secondly, the only reason I didn't speak to Ariel or Juliet is because they were doing more then enough for me and had problems of their own. Third, for Juliet not to call me and ask for an explanation and just "dismiss" me without a chance to even speak felt like such a slap in the face. The last part was Ariel, my friend, mentor, brother and the man who always had my back. Just two weeks prior I wrote him a statement giving him 10% of my income next year as a gift. He didn't even respond. To not call and speak to me like a man first about the situation really hurt.

Whether they want to admit it or not, I helped them grow. Many clients and people they work with now or have worked with in the past were due directly to me. I gave them so much exposure as a whole and really helped to brand them as one of the premier recording studios in New York. When it was all said and done though, all my efforts counted for nothing. I never felt so betrayed in my life, and it would only get worst as time went on.

I didn't say a word publically, until now. You know how crazy it was? I didn't even hear my album till the day of its release. That was the first and last time I listened to it in it's entirety. Many of my verses were off beat, which I was furious about and I was just totally disgusted with the entire process after that point. I just gritted my teeth and smiled to the public though. That project was the most bittersweet achievement of my life and everything associated with it will be burned in my brain forever.

I have no malice or spite towards any of them, but Ariel and Juliet don't exist to me anymore. Everyone else in there I have no issues with. I forgive them for how they treated me but I honestly want nothing to do with them. They wouldn't even give me my hard drive that contained years of my music. In the end I had to have 5 years of work destroyed for my own protection. I can assume why they didn't want to release the music, but I can't defame or slander them publically and it's not even worth speculation. All I know is that chapter of my life is closed.

On the night of my release party at S.O.B's, **NO ONE** showed up from that circle except for Polo Pirate (great dude). Not even Maki. That was the all I needed to see. I have no regrets; business is business as they say right?

Chapter Six: Release

It's ironic. As I write this chapter that The Red Hot Chili Peppers are on repeat in the background. Anthony Kiedis may have single handily saved my career at that point. I almost felt like throwing in the towel but his book, Scar Tissue helped me get through the rest of that year. He helped me realize that I'm not as "crazy" as others may perceive me to be. New Years night I spent alone reading the final chapter of that book and woke up to a new life. Before I go any further though I have to go back a bit to continue the story.

During the promotion of that album I did many things behind the scenes to secure my future. I got my Tax ID first, started working on getting my business license as I moved upstairs to a much larger apartment that would accommodate my future aspirations perfectly. I also found a new passion. Charity.

Remember how I said I was going to magazines talking about my future project and endeavors? One of the people I spoke to was Andy Cohn of Fader. Andy is the best. Good guy, fair, truthful and all around stand up dude. So when he invited me to a charity event they were conducting I didn't hesitate to accept.

The private event was for a program called My Music RX that was created by the Children's Cancer Association. Little did I know, that Rob Stone (one of the Founders of Cornerstone and Fader) had been afflicted with cancer as a young man and music was one of the main reasons he survived. I researched the organization and knew that I had to help.

The first thing I did as an artist was pledge %5 of all my digital sales for the first quarter of 2012 to the organization. I did this in private but Andy asked to read it at the event. I was shy about it honestly (I'm not use to broadcasting things like that) but said it was cool. Anyway I could help I would. After hearing the stories, especially the one of Regina Ellis (the Founder of CCA) I felt compelled to help raise funds and awareness for the charity.

By now I'm sure you can see that I don't speak about many things publically (contrary to popular belief, I'm not really a fan of talking to be honest. It just happens to be part of my job so I do it excessively) and I've revealed many things in this book a lot of you have never known. Here is another secret. My mother was diagnosed with breast cancer and fighting the disease during the entire process of the album and such. That was one of the main reasons why I had to seek professional counseling. I felt like I was losing my mind. Alongside the fact that I had also lost a child (which was another reason why I was in therapy) her and Rob's story resonated with me immensely. So I became an advocate for their campaign and charity.

At this point I could give two sh!ts about my album, and I focused my energy on something positive. Since it was out though, I decided to use the momentum of that project for something good. So with the help of my homie Bobby Greenleaf (another great guy) we created one hundred special T-Shirts for the charity. Every shirt sold we would donate $20 to the cause. I still continue to this day to fight this terrible disease besides them. Not for the accolades, or praise but because if people such as myself don't do it who else would?

Something else interesting happened during that promotional campaign. I was performing at A3C that year and ran into an artist by the name of Catch Lungs. Destiny has a funny way of aligning people, places and things at the right time. Him and me had performed back in '09 at Santos together and he remembered me. He was manning the Akomplice clothing booth and we got to talking. I asked him if was performing at any shows and he told me no, I'm just here to do this. I wouldn't have that.

I invited him to come and freestyle with me at my Okayplayer performance. I don't think many people understand, or rather expect Donny Goines to do certain things. I believe it catches many others in this industry off guard. I didn't ask him for anything nor did I expect anything in return, I just did because he's an MC and should be on stage. I have a habit of doing things such as this. I don't mind sharing the stage, money, tangible items, etc. mainly because certain things are just not that important to me. I had no idea what this would lead to eventually, but the universe is a very strange and mystical place.

Months later, I received an email from a gentleman by the name of Dan Lafferman. He appreciated what I had done for his artist (he managed Catch Lungs) and wanted to me to work with him on his next project. We came to an agreement of $2,500 for me to Executive Produce his album and from that point forward, Ink Different Inc. was born.

Dan had flown Catch down to Atlanta to stay with me (hence the reason for the large space) for a few weeks so we could feel each other out, bounce ideas around and such. I took Catch with me to certain spots, introduced him to some people, let him perform at a New Era event with me and basically just had a good time. Him and me really built a strong rapport, and he started to explain his relationship with his manager Dan (whom I had never met to this day) at the time I would brush off as the typical frustrated artist. I would eventually find out the hard way what he meant.

Dan and me clicked instantly. He presented himself as a person with a lot of financial resources and ambition. I liked him from the very beginning and once Catch went back we started to speak more and more about business. Eventually he decided to invest in my company. I gave him a small percentage in my company for some modest financial backing and we got to work.

In the beginning, everything seemed cool. I liked his vibe and he seemed to really understand the business of music. We built a website, started getting organized and created the movement you now see today. Catch came back down and what started as a plan of him staying a few weeks turned into him staying down for months and moving in. On the backend I finally felt as if I found someone who understood my vision and even upped his percentage based upon his actions. I didn't view him as just an investor, I viewed him more like a business partner and treated him as such.

Now things were starting to flow. I had clients seeking help, which generated income for the business. I also made money from my own brand as an artist and businessman and everything seemed to be headed toward the right direction. As time would go on though I started to notice some things I personally didn't like about him. Now the words Catch has spoken of previously had struck a cord with me, and the notes didn't sound too good.

Chapter 7: Donny the "C.E.O"

Chief Executive Officer. Sounds good on paper right? So, I carried myself as such. I retained the services of an accountant firm, Entertainment Lawyer, Personal Driver, etc. and got to work. I started to buy all the equipment I needed to self-record, opened up business accounts and got all of my paperwork straight. At this point, I was functioning at a high capacity on this business side. I consulted a good friend of mines I'd known for years named Albert Sye to help guide me in the beginning (he recommended Omara Harris, an attorney who would help me acquire my business license and Keisha Perry who would represent me in legal aspects of the entertainment realm). He also provided great insight into the Atlanta scene, business and things of that nature.

I started to maneuver within the city quietly. One other person I had meet during A3C would be a lady named Marie More. Great person and I asked her for advice and such as well. I love her energy. She moderated a panel I was speaking on. After introducing myself to her, we built a great friendship. In fact there are many people down here who would help me navigate the inner workings (which I'm still learning to this day) of this interesting city. Tom, Big O and Jason, Soul Wallace, Summer and Susan of my building, Jay my driver at the time, Roy Garrison, Lil Rod, Hass, Groove, Shika, Artists, Fort Knox and many others.

Once I started to settle down I began to venture into many different things. For instance, I noticed a young man by the name of Ajee in my building. He was very young and seemed lost so I took him under the wing. He asked me to be his mentor and I accepted.

I also started to plan events, Catch's career, business moves and an overall strategy for the next few months. I had one small problem though. Dan. He had begun to question what I would do with the money he was investing into the company. He was also not as "financially stable" as he presented himself to be. This would pose a serious problem as the weeks went on.

Catch and me were butting heads a lot too. We just had different outlooks on music, the world, beliefs and such which is to be expected. We would argue at times and disagree on a lot of things but basically we we're just feeling each other out. During the time he left from the first trip I would meet an interesting woman by the name of Simone Declama. Simone and myself got along great. Can't really explain it. Just natural organics I suppose. Now we all four (Myself, Catch, Ajee & Simone) would start working together towards goals of the company.

I believe Dan was the first to be ousted. After awhile his persistent questioning, not being able to provide for the company or his artist and many other things were just starting to rub me the wrong way. I'm not exactly sure when it happened, but I eventually just told him his services were no longer needed and got rid of him. This is not to say everything in the situation I did was correct, but I can't work under certain pressures at this stage of my career and life and just left a similar situation so this posed a major problem for me. It also posed issues for Catch as well so we both decided to move forward and keep going on.

This left the company with a huge gap to fill. I needed a second in command.

Chapter 8: The Declama Drama

Before I begin this chapter I have to state a disclaimer. I have a pending defamation lawsuit against her so certain facts must be omitted due to the confidentiality of the situation

Simone was an interesting woman. I really loved her creative style and mind. I think she has immense talent and is also a beautiful woman inside and out. We were intimate, which I think played a major factor in the events that would later transpire but she had assured me that they would not conflict. I believed her.

During late February I threw an Atlanta based event for MyMusicRX and The Children's Cancer Association in my building. I partnered up with Conjure liquor (Ludacris's company) and was in talks with Porsche (hence that original commercial my company had created some of you had seen floating around) but my proposal didn't fall through. Also around this time my sister Shakeena had came down to stay with me and I fired Ajee as an intern for the company and no longer would mentor him. Some people need to learn hard lessons (I'm not exempt from this either) and he is one of those types.

Based upon the way Simone had handled the event I believe she was the perfect candidate and gave her the title of C.O.O/Creative Director. I knew from the beginning she wasn't "prepared" for this position but figured I could groom and teach her. I also believed she deserved a chance to do something of this magnitude and wanted to give her a shot.

Let me address a couple of things about myself before I go any further. I am a f#ck up. I will be the first to admit that. I make mistakes constantly and don't try to hide these facts. In almost every situation mentioned in this book I contributed some sort of negative, resistant or childish behavior. I also can be very selfish at times depending on how you view things. I try to be the best human being I can be but obviously I am flawed and hold myself ultimately responsible for almost every situation I put myself in. I can't control (nor do I want to) others, but I can control the way I handle situations and make personal changes to improve. I'm a work in progress and am not trying vilify anyone in this book. All I'm doing is stating the facts and my opinions of things that have occurred in the past year. There are always three sides of every story, and this book represents two of them.

In the beginning, the transitions had seemed to be impossible but eventually we found a groove. Everything seemed to be working the way I had envisioned it would but as the days dragged on various problems behind the scenes had occurred. Mismanagement of funds, failure of certain campaigns, not being able to pay people on time… The best way to explain it in my mind? We were all just a bunch of children in the playground with no adults around. **MANY** mistakes were made and things started to get out of control.

Bills were not being paid, duties were not being fulfilled and many problems I could not foresee arose. Like always though, I just kept on going (notice a constant theme here?) and just addressed the situations as best I could. There were several arguments, too much confusion and not enough order. All of this led me to this point I'm at today.

Many amazing things occurred during this time period though. I secured a booking agent, company to license my music, many major campaigns and clients, made some great friends (Cheryl helped me through many issues) and made it through the first quarter with about 10K profit. Not bad for an upstart business if I do say so myself.

Catch also completed his album "Mermaids & Vampires" (very special thanks to Simon Illi) which is sponsored by several companies and is currently on a pre-promotional tour right now. We even got our own customized tour kicks (check them out below) among other things. Simone though, just wasn't working out due to several different factors so I had to fire her.

Now it's just Catch and me essentially. One thing I've always liked about Catch? He is a survivor, just like myself. He knows how to weather the storm and that's why he will be rewarded to a bountiful feast in the near future. My sister is doing well, working and going to school and I hope she decides to join my company one day. I believe she has amazing potential.

So where does this leave myself? Well I'm doing everything alone and learning lessons the hard way. I haven't reached a full calendar year of my company yet and don't know what to expect, but you know something? It's been one hell of a ride thus far.

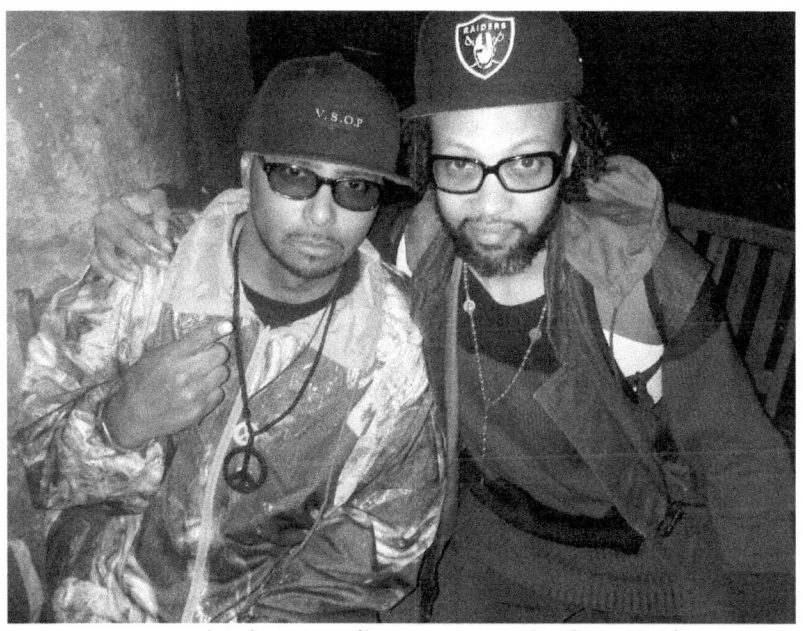
Me and Polo Pirate (he put me in the fly jacket)

MyMusicRX X Fader T-Shirt

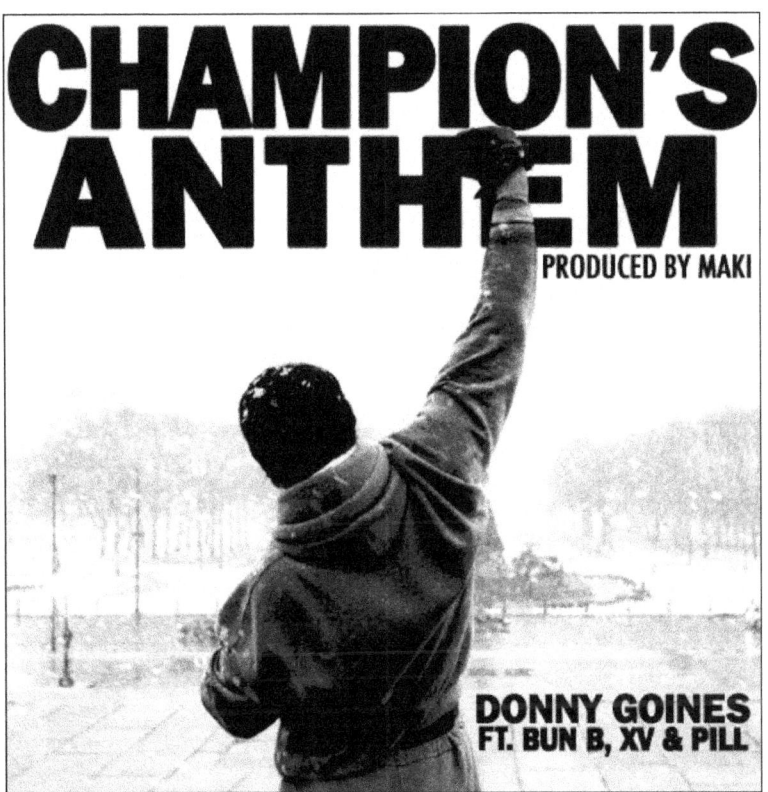
Champion's Anthem

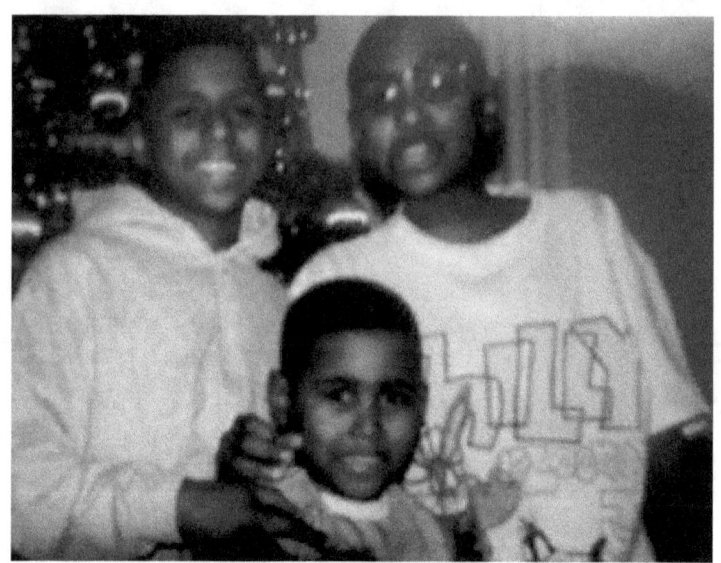

Jonnie, Jason and Myself (I miss those days)

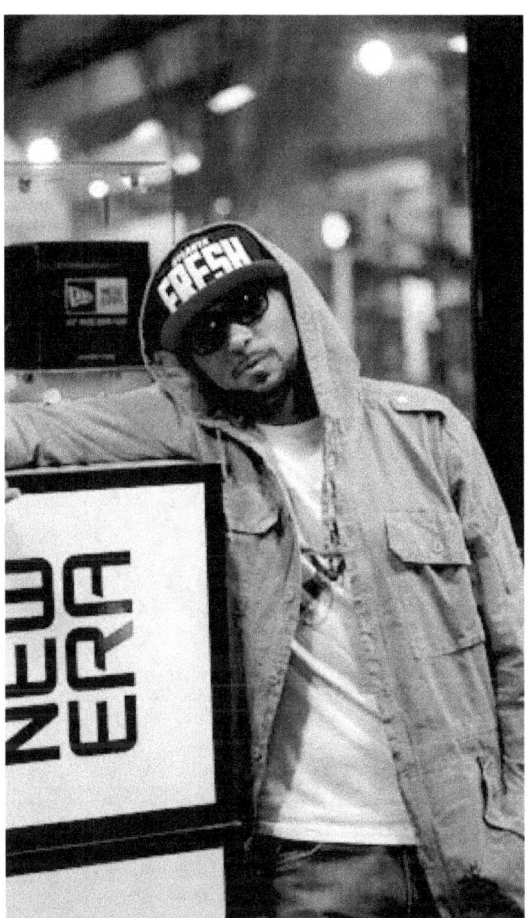

Me at the New Era Flagship Store

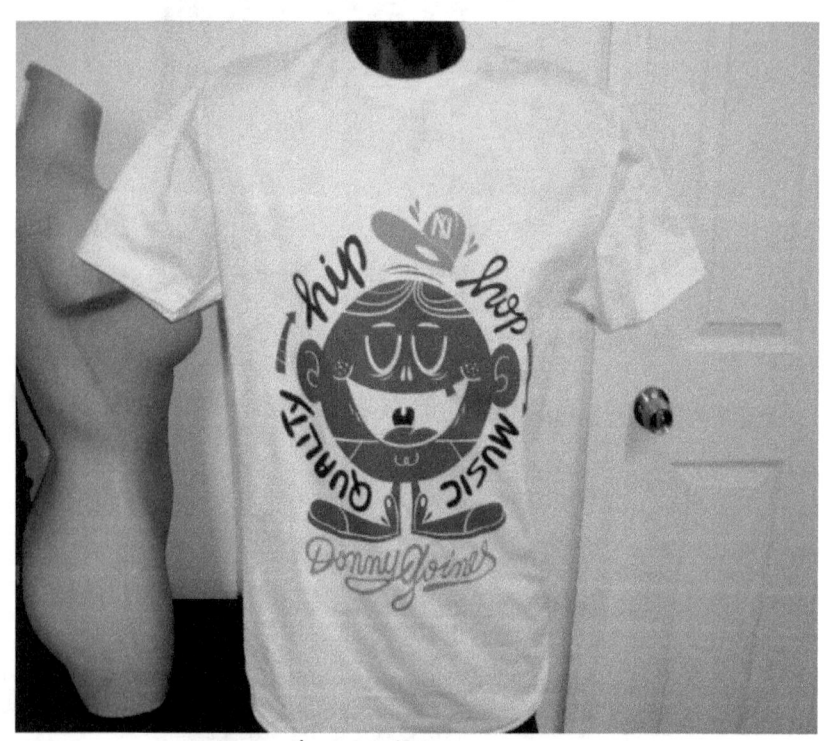

I'm wearing one now

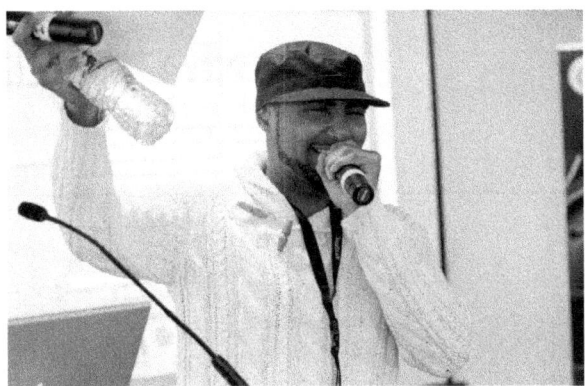

SoundCity New York

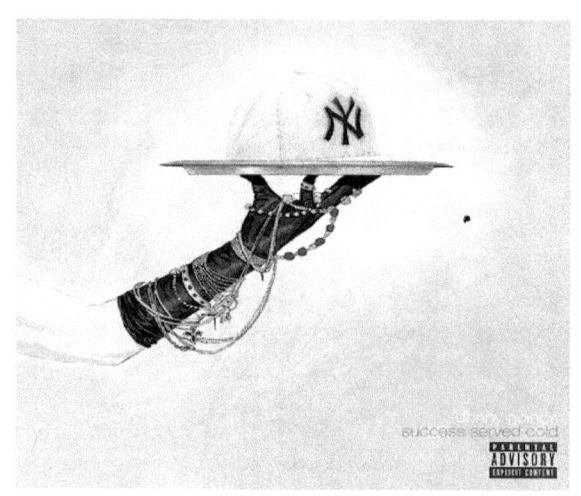

#SSC

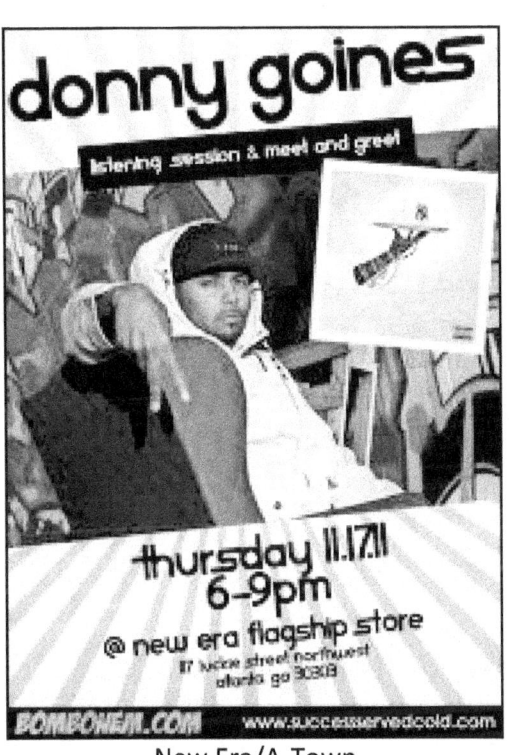

New Era/A-Town

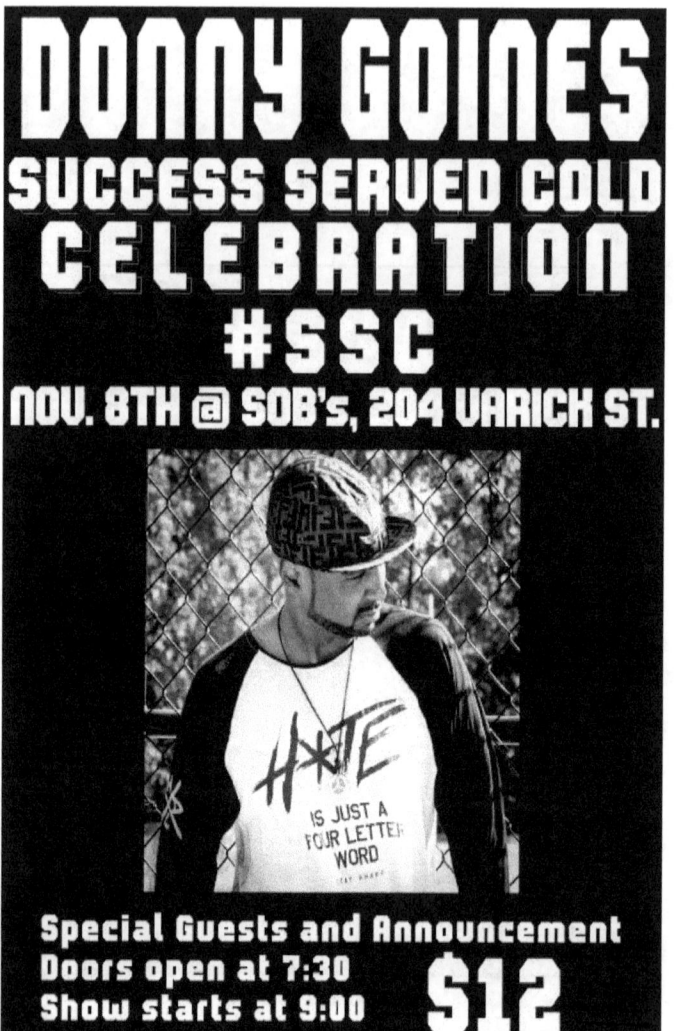

Much Love to SOB's

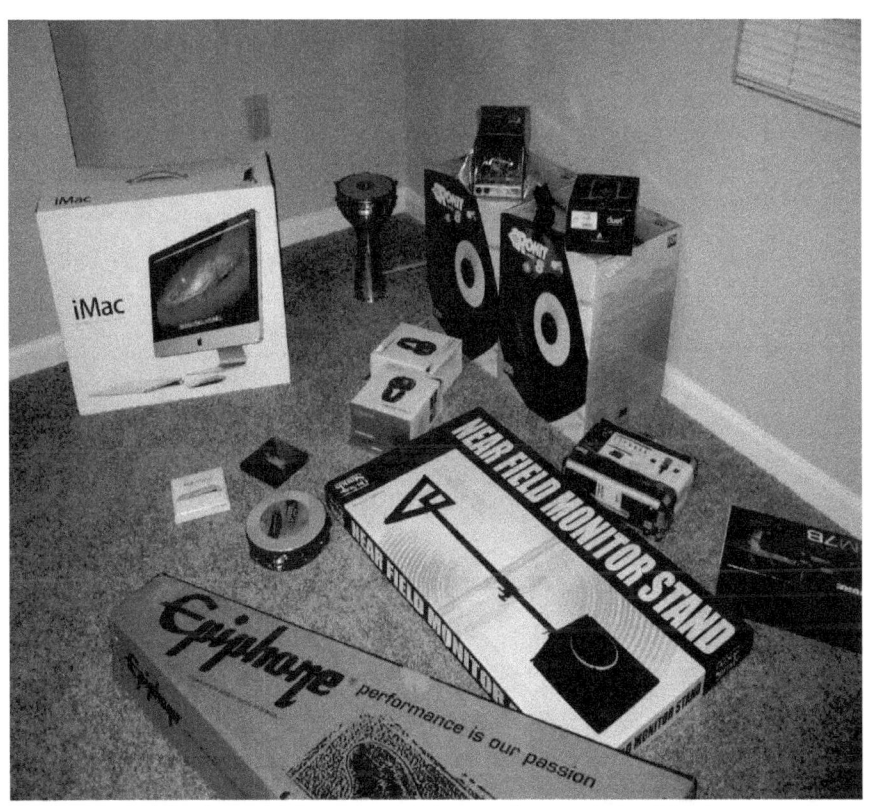

Equipment I never got to use (except the Mac)

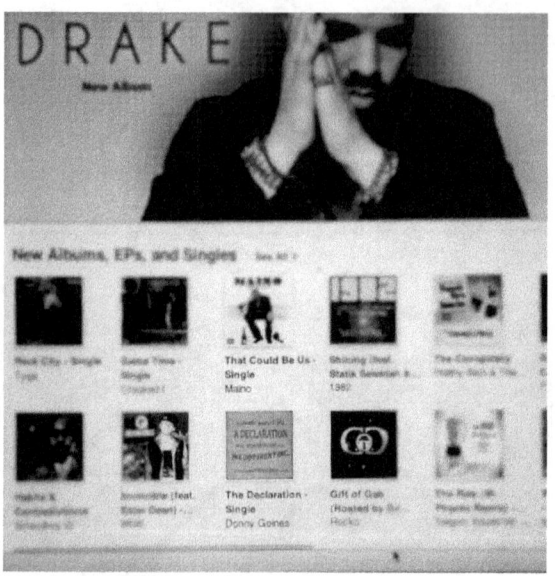

My first placement on iTunes

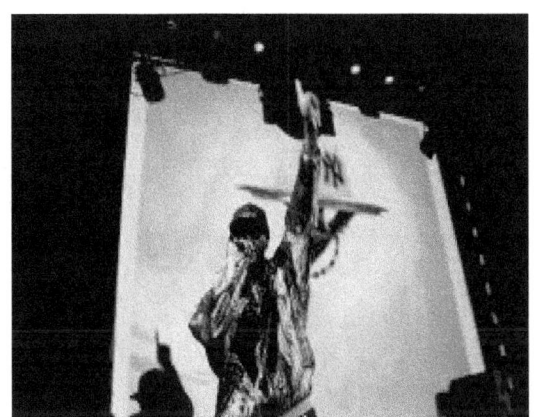
Ich!ban

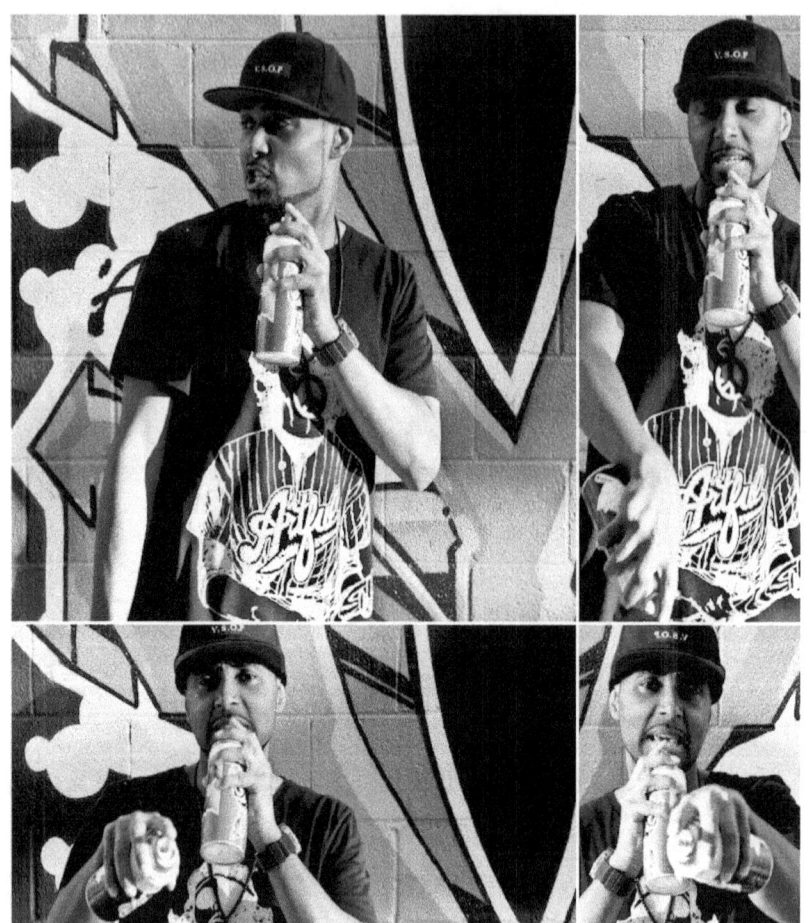

Visual Noise

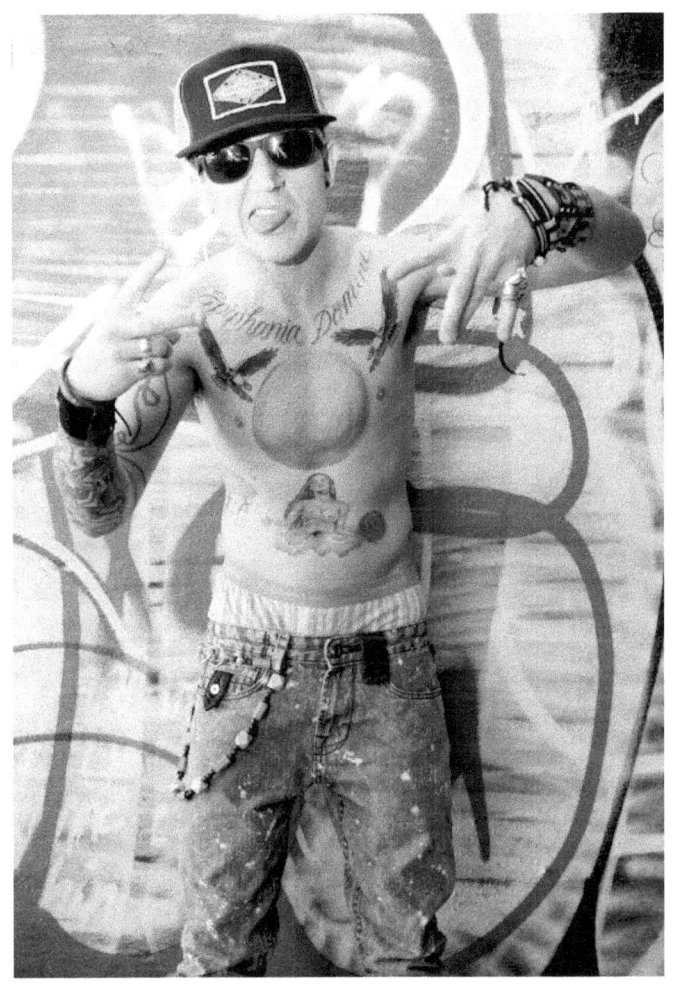

Catch Lungs

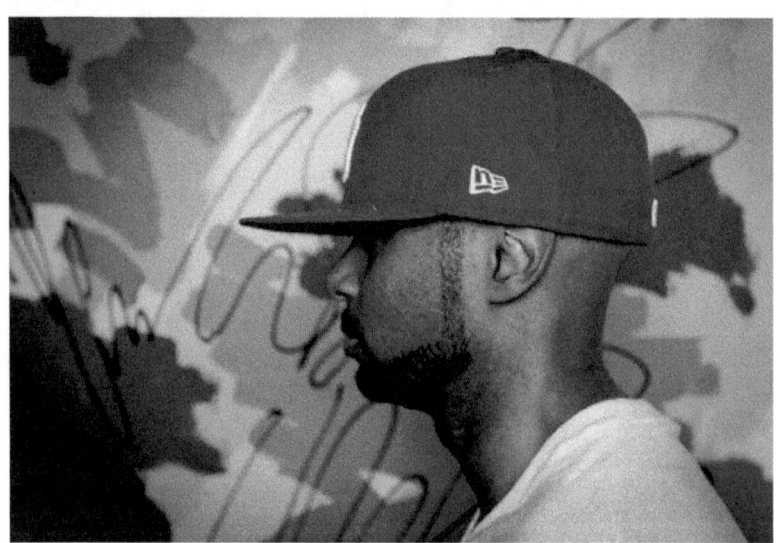

Art in Motion

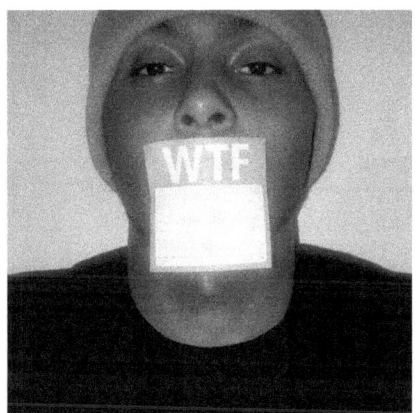

Just a weird picture

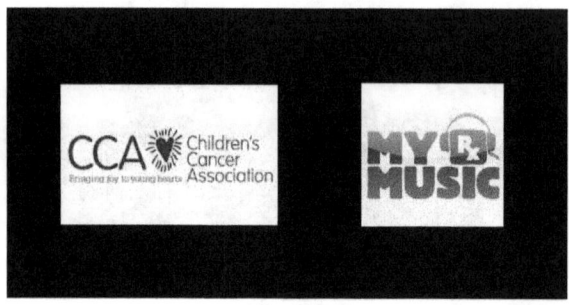

Donate

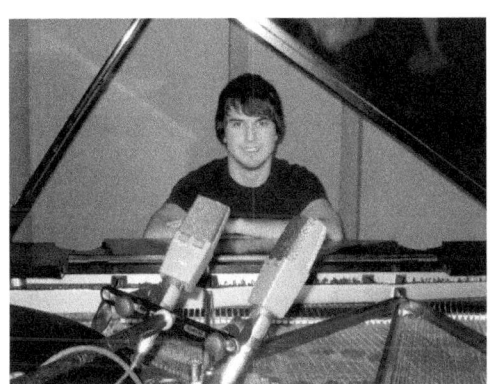

Claude Z

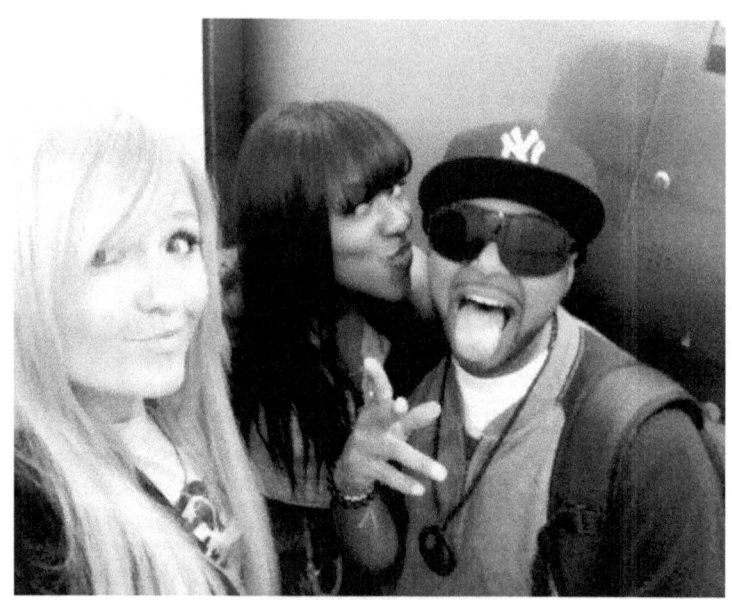

Irena, Tali and Myself

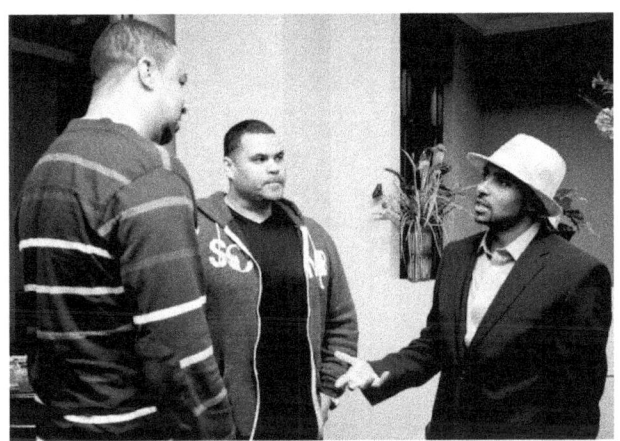

Big Al!

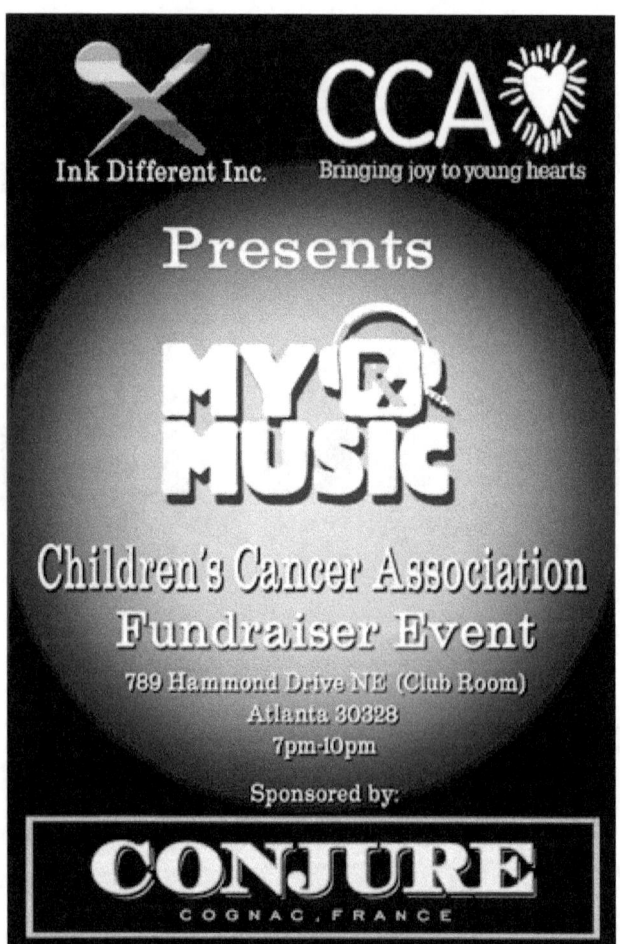

Fun times/Great cause

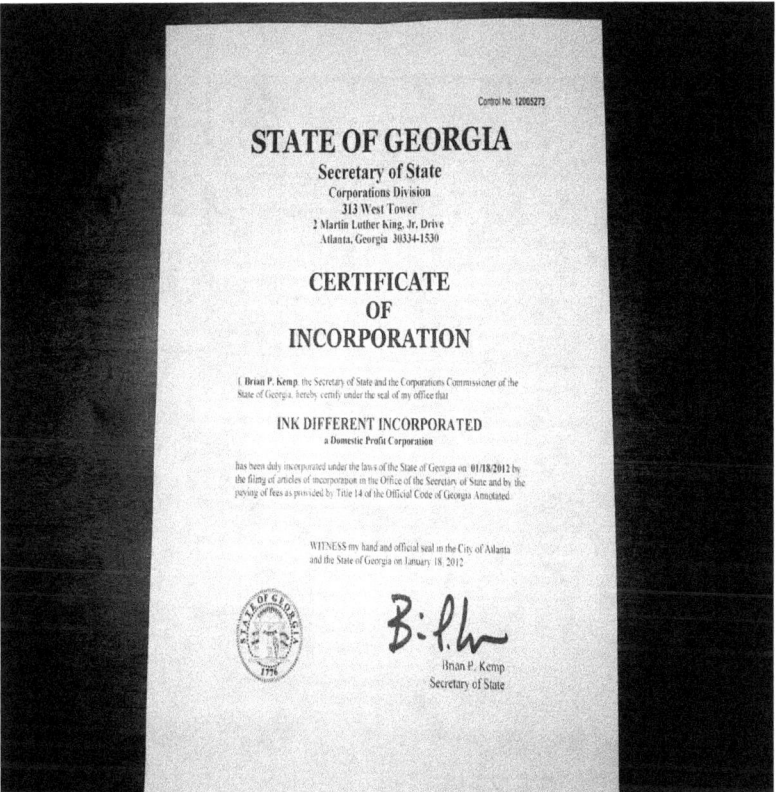

One of my greatest accomplishments thus far

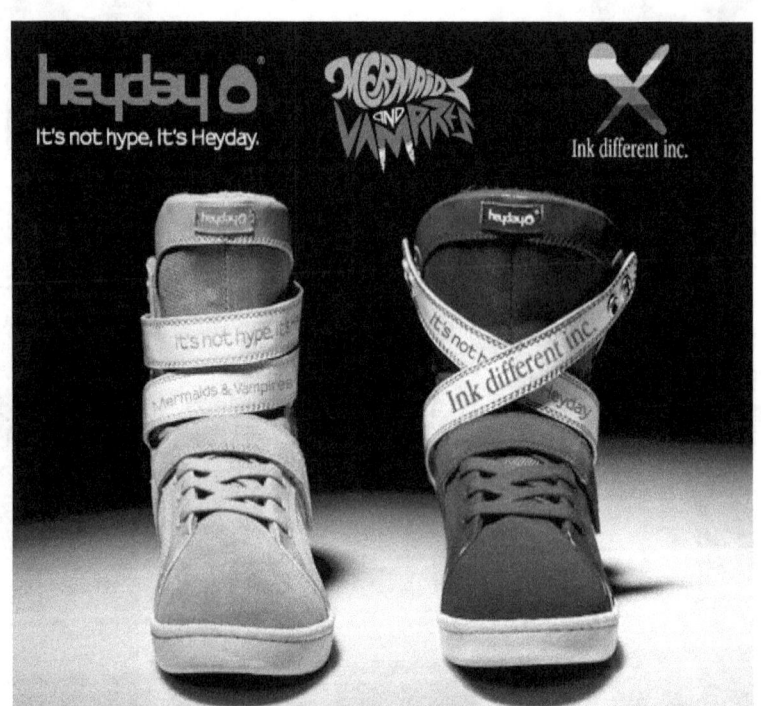

"It's not just hype, It's Heyday"

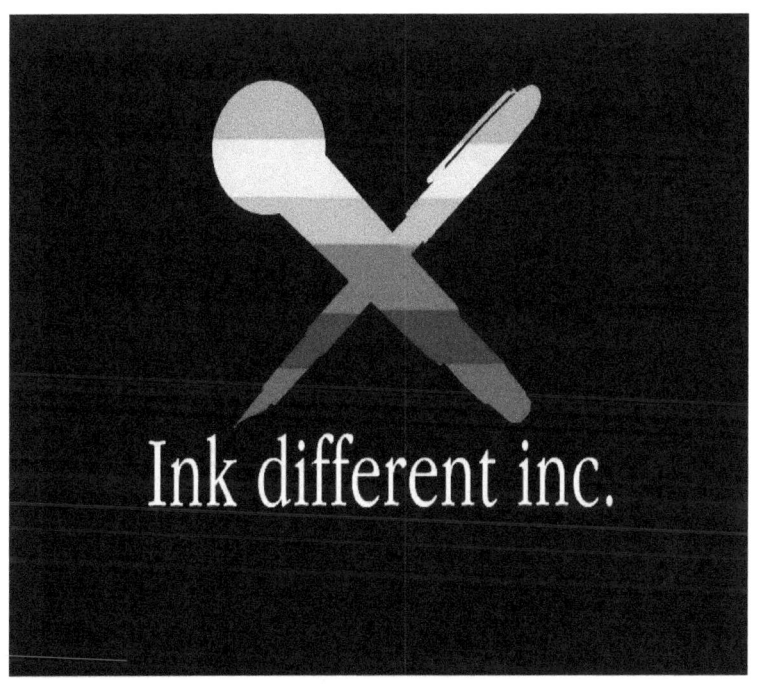

Ink different inc.

The story is just getting started...